MW00877035

First printing – June 2016

CELIBACY

Copyright © 2016 by Jacqueline Guthrie

Published by Lulu

ISBN 978-1-365-20853-9

Printed in the United States of America

Myriam,

You display what this book is about you! I love you smile & kind spirit. Enjoy!

Jacqueline

Contents

I. The Foundation of Celibacy

Chapter 1: Celibacy Defined

Celibacy. What comes to your mind when you hear the word? Is it the image of a nun, who has vowed to remain unmarried, living in a convent full of other women? Does it bring up the stereotype of the homely single woman living alone with her cats? Do you associate the word with boring and "lame"? Do you think those who choose celibacy are people who are unattractive and undesirable? What relationship do celibacy and Christianity have, if any?

I did not know what celibacy meant or what it was all about when I studied the Bible and became a Christian at the age of seventeen. All I knew was that I was lost, and I wanted God. I simply knew that having a relationship with God meant that I could not have sex before marriage, and that the person I married had to be a disciple of Jesus. What I was not aware of at the time were the realities, hardships, and suffering that would come with living that lifestyle day in and day out, year after year.

Now, twenty years later, I know that nothing else has refined my character and strengthened my relationship with God quite like the lifestyle of celibacy. Celibacy is not optional for an unmarried disciple of Jesus, yet living it successfully can seem quite daunting and nearly impossible—but it *is* worth it. I hope to share with you the many lessons I have learned and what I have had to fight through to remain faithful to God through this time, all while still having the hope and desire of marriage burning strongly in my heart. Whatever you believe about celibacy, I hope that by the end of this book you will feel inspired and ready to take on the challenge of living successfully the celibate lifestyle God intended.

Of all the definitions for the word celibacy, the one I like best simply defines it as "the state of being unmarried; single life."[1] According to this definition, anyone who is single or unmarried is celibate. I like this definition because it broadens the scope of what being single means. There is no association with the word "sex" in this definition. Today the word celibacy has become interchangeable with sexual abstinence. Later in the book, we will see from Scripture how sex relates to God, and how that

---

[1] *Webster's Online Dictionary*, s.v. "celibacy," accessed December 23, 2014, http://www.webster-dictionary.org/definition/celibacy.

relationship connects to the single and unmarried. There are so many aspects of the single and unmarried life that have nothing to do with sex.

To successfully live the single life as God intended entails more than simply deciding to abstain from sex. Success is defined as "a favorable or desired outcome; *also*: the attainment of wealth, favor, or eminence."[2] Who does not want to know the secret of how to attain wealth, favor and eminence in their personal life? Amazingly, the world does not equate success with celibacy. The world teaches that success for the single person is having a great career, living in a fancy penthouse, having lots of money and having the most eligible bachelor or bachelorette on your arm. The religious world teaches that success for the unmarried individual—especially the unmarried woman—is found in being a good person, getting married and raising a devout family. However, what does *God* call success?

[God] wants all people to be saved and to come to a knowledge of the truth (1 Timothy 2:4).

The Lord is not slow in keeping his promise, as some understand slowness. Instead he is patient with you, not wanting anyone to perish, but everyone to come to repentance (2 Peter 3:9).

I am the gate; whoever enters through me will be saved. They will come in and go out, and find pasture. The thief comes only to steal and kill and destroy; I have come that they may have life, and have it to the full (John 10: 9–10).

Ultimately, God wants every person of every race, whether single or married, rich or poor, to be saved and come to a knowledge of the truth. God also wants us to have a full life. That desire is why Jesus came. *Success in God's eyes is living life to the full through Jesus and spending eternity with Him.*

Most Christians would agree that God's view of success sounds good. However, for many years in my Christian walk I felt far from being successful. I hated being single. I felt that being single in the Kingdom of God was the furthest thing from any kind of success, and that nothing

---

[2] *Merriam-Webster,* s.v. "success," accessed January 6, 2015, http://www.merriam-webster.com/dictionary/success.

about it was even remotely close to life to the full. As the years went by, all my friends from my college days got married and started families. Then the teens that I mentored got married and started families. I felt more and more like a failure rather than a success story. I felt like the writer of Psalm 73:

> Surely in vain I have kept my heart pure
> and have washed my hands in innocence.
> All day long I have been afflicted,
> and every morning brings new punishments....
> When I tried to understand all this,
> it troubled me deeply
> till I entered the sanctuary of God;
> then I understood. ...
> My flesh and my heart may fail,
> but God is the strength of my heart
> and my portion forever. ...
> But as for me, it is good to be near God.
> I have made the Sovereign Lord my refuge;
> I will tell of all your deeds (from Psalm 73:13–28).

I felt like serving God and being pure was all in vain. I was so unhappy. It was not until I "entered the sanctuary of God" that I understood that living the single life as God intended is truly successful in His eyes, and it *is* possible to live life to the full. I have had to enter that sanctuary numerous times throughout my spiritual journey in order to truly understand the value in doing things God's way. Now I have a story to share and I understand the purpose in all of it.

Before you can discover how to live life to the full celibately, you have to look at the foundations for celibacy. Facing and embracing the realities of singlehood can lead to truly appreciating all that celibacy has to offer in God's design.

Chapter 2: Celibacy and Lordship

In the life of a Christian, one's foundation begins and ends with Jesus. He is the reason for everything we do. He is the chief cornerstone and the only way to salvation. Life to the full is found only in Him and through Him. To gain this life, we have to make Jesus Lord. We have to build our lives on the Scriptures and be committed to Jesus' standard of discipleship.

Celibacy is not just a good idea or a smart moral decision; it is a lordship issue. Jesus' lordship is central in a saving relationship with God: "Therefore let all Israel be assured of this: God has made this Jesus, whom you crucified, both Lord and Messiah" (Acts 2:36). Jesus is Lord, and He must be Lord of every area of your life, no matter what phase of life you are in. For better or worse, in sickness or health, for richer or poorer, whether single or married, barren or with children, Jesus has to be Lord.

Lordship has become an unpopular subject for many. Everyone wants Jesus to be their Savior, but very few want Jesus to be their Lord. Jesus asks in Luke 6:46, "'Why do you call me, 'Lord, Lord', and do not do what I say?" Jesus' expectation is that with Him as our Lord, we will do what He says. The word *lord* is defined as "one having power and authority over others,"[3] or in other words, one who is a master, a ruler, a king. Is Jesus ruling your unmarried life? Is He calling all the shots in your life?

Lordship involves discipleship. Discipleship is following Jesus and walking the walk. God's standard of commitment is complete and total devotion to Him. If I am unable to be committed to God, then I can never be truly committed to a man. God's expectation for a relationship with Him are high:

> Large crowds were traveling with Jesus, and turning to them he said: "If anyone comes to me and does not hate father and mother, wife and children, brothers and sisters—yes, even their own life—such a person cannot be my disciple. And whoever does not carry their cross and follow me cannot be my disciple....

---

[3] *Merriam-Webster*, s.v. "lord," accessed January 6, 2015, http://www.merriam-webster.com/dictionary/lord.

In the same way, those of you who do not give up everything you have cannot be my disciples" (Luke 14:25–33).

Jesus lays out a high call for commitment in this passage. He makes a distinction between those who travel with Him and those who follow Him as His disciples. In this passage, large crowds were "traveling with Jesus." This Scripture implies that these people believed in Him and chose to spend their time with Him. Jesus, however, expected more from them than just hanging around. Jesus wanted them to be totally sold out for Him. Just because they were hanging around Him did not mean that they were His followers.

What is the difference between a traveler and a follower? Their commitment to Jesus being Lord. A follower puts Jesus first in his life, making Him the weightiest relationship and priority. He loves Jesus more than anyone else, more than even his own life. A follower carries his cross and has given up everything for Jesus. A traveler, on the other hand, is not fully committed and invested in Jesus being the main priority. A traveler comes and goes when it is convenient; he is visiting and exploring. A traveler can leave whenever he wants to—and he probably will when times get tough. A few years ago, when the war in Iraq had just started, there was a huge push to get Americans citizens traveling in the country out ASAP; American soldiers, on the other hand, were getting ready to head into battle. If you have a traveler's mindset when it comes to being with Jesus, you will escape to save your own interests when the spiritual war begins. But a follower, like a soldier, is always there: good or bad, thick or thin.

Jesus gives us insight here into three things that hinder total commitment:

1. We are unwilling to value Him more than our other relationships and our lives.

2. We are unwilling to carry the cross.

3. We are unwilling to give up everything, including our freedom and our choices.

Take some time to examine your own life, and ask yourself if any of the reasons above hinder your commitment to God and your relationship with Him. Are you still following Jesus, or have you taken on the traveler's mindset? Maybe you go to church every week and are around the body of Christ, but have stopped truly following Jesus in your heart. As single Christians, we have to decide to be all in with God or walk away from Him. That all-in decision means we are followers of Christ even if we never get married or live the life we dreamed of.

When I first read the lordship passage in Luke 6, I was totally amazed by Jesus telling people they *could not* be His disciples! I had always thought that Jesus accepted everyone, but now I realized that Jesus would only accept those who were willing to agree to His standard of discipleship. Throughout my twenty years as a disciple, it has been a fight to remain true to Jesus' standard of commitment. Jesus will not compromise, and neither can we.

I have gone through many hard times. I have wanted to throw in the towel and go find a man to be with. It is often hard waiting on God to work! However, He is always faithful, and always gives me just enough faith to keep me going. My commitment to live for God is the foundation for my way of living. Celibacy is one of the outcomes of making Jesus my Lord. Everything else about celibacy is meaningless if we do not have lordship on straight.

When I stood in the waters of baptism and said my good confession, "Jesus is Lord," I had no idea that I would have to say that confession many times throughout my journey with God. Just as I had to wrestle with things in my character and deal with my sin in order to get baptized, I have had to continue to wrestle in order to stay surrendered to doing things God's way. I continue daily to make and live the confession that Jesus is Lord.

The reason I became a Christian and made Jesus Lord was because I wanted God, plain and simple. I wanted to be right with Him. I did not want to continue to live this life without Him, and I wanted to make it to heaven. The end goal of this life is not about having a great marriage or even having a great life (in many ways we might like to define "great"), but about making it to heaven. For the unmarried disciple, the life of sexual abstinence is not just a great suggestion; it is God's expectation for all single believers. *Celibacy is motivated and fueled by the love of Christ.* By living out this conviction, we can experience the full life God wants to give us.

Chapter 3: Celibacy and the Bible

All Scripture is God-breathed and is useful for teaching, rebuking, correcting and training in righteousness, so that the servant of God may be thoroughly equipped for every good work (2 Timothy 3:16–17).

Reading this Scripture for the first time was eye-opening. It made me aware that the Bible was not just some words thrown together by man, but the very words of God. What was even more astounding to me was that the Bible was described as useful. For me, the Bible would definitely not be on my list of useful things for daily living. Its greatest use to me was as a decorative piece of décor.

When I committed to making Jesus Lord and chose celibacy, I realized that I needed teaching, correcting and training in how to live this lifestyle. I needed to be equipped, and the Scriptures were the source. We cannot live the life God intends without being committed to the Scriptures. If Jesus' expectation as our Lord is that we will do what He says, then we must find His directives in the Bible.

When talking about celibacy, especially sexual abstinence, many people (even you) may ask, "Did God really say we could not have sex before marriage? Did God really say you have to be so super-committed? Did God really say...?" You fill in the blank. I am a firm believer that at the end of the day everyone should know why they do what they do. This is called *building your own convictions*.

So what does God really say about celibacy and sexual abstinence? We will address that question by looking at the Bible. However, to truly put our faith in the Bible, we have to believe that it is the inspired word of God, believing that it holds the keys to life and has the power to change our lives. 1 Timothy 4:16 says, "Watch your life and doctrine closely. Persevere in them, because if you do, you will save both yourself and your hearers." Your doctrine is whatever you hold as your belief code or your standard. Your belief code is whatever you choose to believe is true. So, what is truth?

Jesus answered, "I am the way and *the truth* and the life..." (John 14:6, emphasis added).

In the beginning was the Word, and the Word was with God, and the Word was God. ...The Word became flesh and made his dwelling among us. We have seen his glory, the glory of the one and only Son, who came from the Father, full of grace and *truth* (John 1:1, 14, emphasis added).

To the Jews who had believed him, Jesus said, "*If you hold to my teaching*, you are really my disciples. *Then you will know the truth*, and the truth will set you free" (John 8:31–32, emphasis added).

Jesus is the truth, and His teachings lead to truth. Holding to God's word will help us to know Jesus and ultimately to know the truth, which Jesus promises will set us free. The Bible, according to Psalm 119, is perfect, trustworthy, right, radiant, enduring, sure and altogether righteous. It is important to have a solid conviction about the validity of the Scriptures if that is what you claim to be your doctrine.

You may be saying to yourself, "Duh—this is an obvious point to make in a Christian book." But many Christians today question and doubt in their heart of hearts the validity of the Scriptures, as a whole or at least in certain parts. As a result, they have a hard time making it the standard in their lives and holding to its doctrine. Many think that some of the teachings in the Scriptures are outdated and really are not applicable in this day and age. Biblical teachings on sexual abstinence, modesty and submission are just a few doctrines that some Christian women really do not believe or agree with in their hearts. We may try to explain away what God is saying on these controversial topics, or water down His words to suit our needs. But what are you basing your moral and life decisions on? Why do you do what you do?

Another reason to be solidly grounded in the Scriptures is that many people will question you about why you have chosen a celibate way of living. I have heard the whole gamut of responses from friends and family when it comes to my lifestyle. They have told me that I do not have to be so intense and that God understands, that God loves me and wants me to be happy. I have heard things like, "If you love the person, having sex with them is all right." What has helped me to stand firm in this decision to live purely has been my commitment to living by the truth, the Bible. God's word helps me make decisions that are based on truth. Too often people tend to make decisions based on their own understanding or on what society, friends and family say is acceptable; however, they never ask the question "What does God have to say?"

Now there are many people, Christian and non-Christian alike, who think celibacy has no impact on our salvation. The Scriptures clearly teach that no one who lives another lifestyle than that commanded in the Bible should expect to inherit the kingdom of God (1 Corinthians 6:9–10, Galatians 5:19–21). What is your personal conviction on the subject? Ultimately, have you made the Bible the standard in your life? Too many Christians do not rely on the word of God to guide their decisions, so it does not change their day-to-day lives.

Another benefit of being grounded in the Scriptures is that they will help you not to make emotional decisions and will provide clarity in regard to morality. Christians love to say things like, "The Spirit told me to do this" or "The Spirit told me to do that," and that is fine. But what about truth? Jesus tells us what God is looking for:

"Yet a time is coming and has now come when the *true worshipers* will worship the Father *in the Spirit and in truth*, for they are the kind of worshipers the Father seeks. God is spirit, and *his worshipers must worship in the Spirit and in truth*" (John 4:23–24, emphasis added).

Spirit *and* truth: both are indispensable to worshiping God. You cannot worship God only in the Spirit or only in truth. Truth and the Spirit are both important in making moral decisions. If you feel the Spirit is telling you to do something, is it consistent with the truth found in the Bible? If it cannot be backed up by the Scriptures, it is more likely you are hearing your feelings and opinions, and not the Spirit of God. I have found that a good litmus test to show whether what I am thinking is from God is to ask myself, "Are there several Scriptures that support this decision?"

Ultimately, in choosing the life of abstinence you must believe in your soul that it is right and true, basing your truth on the Scriptures and not your opinions or feelings. You must know that the key to success lies in the Word of God. If you ground your life and decisions on the Bible, you will discover the full life that God desires to give you.

Chapter 4: Undivided Devotion

> I would like you to be free from concern. An unmarried man is concerned about the Lord's affairs—how he can please the Lord. But a married man is concerned about the affairs of this world—how he can please his wife—and his interests are divided. An unmarried woman or virgin is concerned about the Lord's affairs: Her aim is to be devoted to the Lord in both body and spirit. But a married woman is concerned about the affairs of this world—how she can please her husband. I am saying this for your own good, not to restrict you, but that you may live in a right way in undivided devotion to the Lord (1 Corinthians 7:32–35).

When I first read this I was confused. Was God saying getting married was wrong? That married people are not called to the same standard of undivided devotion to the Lord? It is clear from Jesus' call of discipleship in the Gospels that He was speaking to all. Whoever does not give up everything they have cannot be His disciples. The call for ALL is undivided devotion to the Lord and concern about the Lord's affairs.

The reality, though, is that married people have additional responsibilities and concerns that will compete with undivided devotion to the Lord. This passage in 1 Corinthians discusses two areas in which an unmarried woman should have undivided devotion: her body and her spirit. We will look more closely at these two areas in the following chapters, but first we want to consider some other noteworthy things this Scripture mentions.

The first is to be "free from concern." It is interesting that the appeal that Paul makes to those who are unmarried comes from his desire for them not to be burdened with concern. When I think of being free from concern, what comes to mind is freedom from worries and responsibilities, a freedom to explore all of life's adventures unrestrictedly. This freedom is a big part of the life that God has intended for the unmarried/single person. God wants us to use this time free from restriction.

Now, having this freedom does not mean we should be irresponsible, or suggest that we will not have troubles in this life. Jesus said that each day has enough trouble of its own (Matthew 6:24). But the reality for many who are unmarried is that this is the most time we will ever have available. For many years I unwisely wasted time worrying about my single status, rather than making the most of it. Being single, I have no one else to really be concerned about except me.

However, God is not advocating freedom from having a purpose. He states in Galatians 5:13 that we should use our freedom to serve others. Because we do not have added responsibilities beyond ourselves, this time should be centered on God and God's affairs. The only exception would be single mothers or caregivers. The call is still for undivided devotion, but people in those roles do have the added responsibility of caring for children or aging relatives.

The second thing to note in 1 Corinthians 7 is how an unmarried woman is "concerned about the Lord's affairs." See how some women put this principle into practice when they were with Jesus:

> **After this, Jesus traveled about from one town and village to another, proclaiming the good news of the kingdom of God. The Twelve were with him, and also some women who had been cured of evil spirits and diseases: Mary (called Magdalene) from whom seven demons had come out; Joanna the wife of Chuza, the manager of Herod's household; Susanna; and many others. These women were helping to support them out of their own means (Luke 8:1–3).**

These women made a personal decision to follow Jesus and support Him out of their own means. This choice was their personal ministry, and they sacrificed for it and invested in it. To my knowledge, all of these women were single except for Joanna. They had the time to be able to travel with Jesus from town to town. If they had husbands and small children to take care of, they would have been unable to go on this adventure, spend this incredible time with Jesus, and see Him on such a personal level.

Throughout the Bible, we see examples of single women doing powerful things for God: Ruth; Jephthah's daughter; Martha and Mary. Another powerful example of single women who did great things for the Kingdom is Phillip's daughters, all of whom prophesied. Talk about dynamic women for God!

Singlehood can be the time to explore the things you would like to do while glorifying God every step of the way. Use the time to be a missionary, go back to school and further your education, go visit other countries, and serve the poor and needy. Now can be the time to write a book, start your own business, or purchase a home. All these things can bring Him glory.

God has given each of us the personal ministry of helping others come to know Him. Seeking and saving the lost is being about the Lord's affairs (Matthew 28:18-20). Are you known as a single who is concerned about the Lord's affairs? Are you sacrificing and investing in your singles' ministry? How is your personal ministry going? Are you using the talents and gifts that God has given you to minister to others, to advance His kingdom and to bring Him glory?

Too often in the church, single women feel that they do not have a significant role in building God's kingdom. Growing up in the faith, I saw very few role models of dynamic single women who were making any impact in the church. All I saw were married women writing books, married women speaking at conferences—and married women leading singles' ministries! I remember at one time thinking that the only role for me in the church was working in the children's ministry. I thought to myself, *"Why is it that I can advance in leadership in worldly careers, but in the church I am limited in what I can do for God?"* Boy, was I out of touch!

It was not until I moved to Atlanta, Georgia in my mid-twenties that I got to see God using single women in a very powerful way to build up His church. This example was something I needed to see: *single* women leading the women's singing ministry, *single* women leading a chemical recovery group, *single* women leading a sexual purity group and (at the time) a *single* woman powerfully leading our singles ministry.

The sky is the limit with God; anything is possible with Him. He wants you to use your talents for Him. Whatever you are passionate about or have a heart for, use it to glorify God. Decide to build up the ministry where God has you. Oftentimes as single women we can get overly concerned about the affairs of this world—our pleasures, our careers, our appearances, and our relationship status. Desiring these things is not wrong, but the point of the Scripture in 1 Corinthians 7 is that as single people—specifically single women—God wants us to be devoted to Him in body and spirit, to be free from concern and to be about His affairs.

Now let us look more closely at what it means to be devoted to God in body and in spirit.

Chapter 5: Undivided Devotion in Body

At seventeen, when I first started seeking God and attending Bible studies, I knew nothing about sexual abstinence. During my Bible studies, we discussed being pure, specifically in relation to sex. It was a new concept for me, with new terminology. The words "purity" and "being pure" were not in my usual vocabulary, and I had never really heard them in connection to a romantic relationship. I had never known anyone who had waited until marriage to have sex. So, like many of us, I had to build my understanding of God's design for sex and sexuality from scratch.

Here are some general definitions of purity:

1. The condition or quality of being pure; freedom from anything that debases, contaminates, pollutes, etc.: *the purity of drinking water.*
2. Freedom from any admixture or modifying addition.
3. Ceremonial or ritual cleanness.
4. Freedom from guilt or evil; innocence.[4]

What stands out to me is the word *freedom*. This word comes up in several variations of the definition. God wants us to be free! Purity brings freedom—freedom from sin, guilt, blame, fault and imperfection. Sexual purity makes us free!

But dealing with the sexual passions we all feel can make sexual purity seem daunting and impossible. I will examine some practical ways of dealing with this later; however, first I want to look specifically at the issue of sexual purity, and how to find the freedom it provides. Let us start by identifying the *opposite* of sexual purity: impurity. The Bible provides some insights into what exactly impurity is:

It is God's will that you should be sanctified: that you should avoid sexual immorality; that each of you should learn to control your own body in a way that is holy and honorable, not in passionate lust like the pagans, who do not know God; and that in this matter no one should wrong or take advantage of a brother or sister. The Lord will punish all those who commit

---

[4] *Dictionary.com,* s.v. "purity," accessed January 8, 2015, http://dictionary.reference.com/browse/purity

such sins, as we told you and warned you before. For God did not call us to be impure, but to live a holy life (1 Thessalonians 4:3–7).

Do not be deceived: Neither the sexually immoral nor idolaters nor adulterers nor men who have sex with men [...] will inherit the kingdom of God (1 Corinthians 6:9–10).

The body, however, is not meant for sexual immorality but for the Lord, and the Lord for the body. By his power God raised the Lord from the dead, and he will raise us also. Do you not know that your bodies are members of Christ himself? Shall I then take the members of Christ and unite them with a prostitute? Never! Do you not know that he who unites himself with a prostitute is one with her in body? For it is said, "The two will become one flesh." But whoever is united with the Lord is one with him in spirit. Flee from sexual immorality. All other sins a person commits are outside the body, but whoever sins sexually, sins against their own body. Do you not know that your bodies are temples of the Holy Spirit, who is in you, whom you have received from God? You are not your own; you were bought at a price. Therefore, honor God with your bodies (1 Corinthians 6:13–20).

The acts of the flesh are obvious: sexual immorality, impurity [...] (Galatians 5:19).

Marriage should be honored by all, and the marriage bed kept pure, for God will judge the adulterer and all the sexually immoral (Hebrews 13:4).

It is God's will that you should be sanctified: that you should avoid sexual immorality; that each of you should learn to control your own body in a way that is holy and honorable, not in passionate lust like the pagans, who do not know God; and that in this matter no one should wrong or take advantage of a brother or sister. The Lord will punish all those who commit such sins, as we told you and warned you before. For God did not call us to be impure, but to live a holy life (1 Thessalonians 4:3–7).

> But among you there must not be even a hint of sexual immorality, or of any kind of impurity, or of greed, because these are improper for God's holy people (Ephesians 5:3).

To sum up, these Scriptures gives us very clear instructions as to what is considered sexual impurity: sex outside of marriage, with "sex" including anything having to do with our bodies; anything that hints of sexuality, such as French kissing, pornography, lust, sexual fantasies and masturbation; homosexuality.

We might conclude from looking at these Scriptures that sexual purity is confining and controlling instead of liberating. Most of us live in societies where almost anything goes. We think, "If it feels good, it cannot possibly be bad." Choosing to give the Lord the undivided devotion of my body, I had to embrace what the Scriptures taught about sexual purity. 1 Corinthians 6:19 compares our bodies to a temple. When we sin sexually, we actually desecrate our bodies and cheapen their value. When I think of a temple, I imagine sacred, precious, priceless and peaceful scenes. That is how God views our bodies and how He wants us to treat them. We should treat our bodies with the utmost respect and care, and anyone else's access to our bodies must be exclusively within marriage.

Make no mistake: *choosing sexual abstinence is choosing to serve God with our bodies' undivided devotion.* Abstinence brings freedom from sin, guilt and blame. Impurity is like an infection, and an infection always brings pain. Sex, according to the Scriptures, is meant to stay within the confines of marriage: "the two will become one flesh" (Genesis 2:24). By engaging in any kind of sexual activity with someone who is not your spouse, you are sinning sexually, against God and against your own body.

How many of us have had regrets or felt defeated, dirty and used after sleeping with someone we barely knew? Or maybe you have been with someone you loved in a relationship that did not work out, and you felt like you gave away the best of you for nothing. We must always keep in the forefront of our minds the things that we know are right according to the Scriptures. We cannot underestimate the call for obedience. Undivided devotion to the Lord in body is a call to uphold God's standard for how He wants us to treat our bodies—His temple.

19

Chapter 6: Undivided Devotion in Spirit

Jesus replied: "'Love the Lord your God with all your heart and with all your soul and with all your mind.' This is the first and greatest commandment." (Matthew 22:37)

God's desire is for singles to be committed to Him not only in body but also with all of our souls. When it comes to choosing to keep our bodies sexually pure and waiting until marriage for sexual relations, many people choose to do so for reasons that have nothing to do with God. Certain cultural and societal norms, fear of pregnancy, fear of getting hurt and fear of STDs are just a few powerfully motivating reasons why some choose to abstain from sex. But choosing celibacy for God is different. Choosing to be undivided in devotion to God in spirit means making a personal decision and commitment to love God and be faithful to Him only, no matter what, for better or worse. When you commit your heart and soul to someone, they have all of you. This type of devotion goes beyond duty or questions of right and wrong; it brings undivided allegiance and loyalty which comes from your desire to love God and Him only!

Judges 11 depicts the inspiring but tragic story of a nameless young single woman who is simply referred to as Jephthah's daughter. This young woman displayed a strong allegiance and devotion to God even at the expense of her own life. From her story we can glean some insight into what it looks like to have an undivided devotion in spirit.

Her father, Jephthah, made a rash vow to God when he said that he would sacrifice the first thing that came from his house if God gave him victory over his enemies. God kept His part and provided the victory. But the first "thing" that came out of Jephthah's house was his daughter. Now both Jephthah and his daughter had a difficult decision to make regarding the vow. And in the end this young woman chose to see a vow to God fulfilled, even though she was not the one who made the vow— she was willing to sacrifice her life rather than allow God to be dishonored.

First, we see that she was a pledge keeper. Do you realize that when you said "Jesus is Lord" in the waters of baptism, you made a pledge to God to live for Him? As disciples of Jesus, our first pledge and dedication is to Christ (1 Timothy 5:11–12). Being a pledge keeper requires you to be a person who is serious about keeping a vow to the Lord. If you said, "Jesus is Lord," and now want to renege on the deal because it is too tough, then your devotion has turned to some other thing or some other person.

Second, we see that Jephthah's daughter was willing to physically lay down her life for God. Even though her story is a rare exception in the Scriptures, since God never commanded His people to sacrifice their children nor did He ever take delight in human sacrifice, her willingness to bear up under the unjust suffering placed on her because she was conscious of God is truly commendable (1 Peter 2:19). Romans 12 states that offering ourselves as a living sacrifice is our spiritual act of worship. Having undivided devotion in spirit means serving the Lord by offering ourselves to God daily because we are so grateful for God's mercy.

What does that look like? I think of the sinful woman who washed Jesus' feet in Luke 7. She gave *all* of herself to serve Jesus. She used her tears and her hair to wash and dry His feet. She used her body in bowing low to honor Him. She did not care who was watching or who was around. She worshiped Him with all of her heart. When we offer ourselves to God as she did, it means we deny ourselves and take up our crosses daily and follow Jesus (Luke 9:23). We use our hands, our feet, and our hearts to worship God and serve the body of Christ.

The sinful woman also broke a very expensive alabaster jar of perfume, worth a year's wages, to let Jesus know how valuable He really was to her. Undivided devotion in spirit comes from a heart of gratitude for God's mercy. Do you remember your days in the world: the tears, the misery, the anxiety, the emptiness and the thought of knowing you were separated from God and going to hell? I remember feeling extremely terrified when I realized that God was not with me. I felt utterly alone and feared God's wrath. When the kindness of God gave me a second chance to make amends with Him, there was nothing I would not have done and nothing I would not have given up to be right with God. I wanted God, and I wanted Him badly.

Despite all the ups and downs in my journey with God, He is still the one I want. Personal lordship, discipleship and having the Word as your standard can seem so uncompromising if you forget God's grace and mercy. Being grateful for my salvation and for God's love is what helps me to continue to run this race of celibacy and undivided devotion to God in both body and spirit. Now that we have examined the case for celibacy based on Scriptures, let us address the realities that come with this way of life.

II. Facing the Realities of Celibacy

Chapter 7: Flying Solo and the Fear of Being Alone

The first reality of being single is being alone. One of the major reasons so many people fail at living the single life as God intended it is that they are not okay with being alone. Sexual abstinence is not the norm nowadays, and certainly not popular or mainstream. Whenever you decide to take an action that is out of the mainstream of popularity, you have to be willing to stand alone, to *be* alone. This choice requires character, which is defined as "moral strength; integrity."[5]

When Martin Luther King, Jr. chose to take a stand for equality, his dream was not mainstream or popular. Many opposed him, and in the end it cost him his life. Jesus chose to reform society, bring new teachings and take a stand for God. He was opposed by the religious leaders of His day, and His beliefs cost Him His life. These men demonstrated character.

Do you believe that celibacy is right for you, based on the word of God? Are you willing to be alone for a long period of time and even die alone for what you believe is right? This decision has been the biggest struggle I have had to face in my walk of celibacy. I have been a single woman for the last twenty years and have not had a boyfriend during that time. I am in my late thirties, and my biological clock has been ticking loudly for a while now. My greatest desire is to get married, and my convictions are being tested. To be a man or woman who succeeds at remaining pure until marriage requires character. To take a stand for what you believe, no matter what you suffer or what cost you have to pay, demands character.

The fear of being alone is a very real cost to count in being celibate for Jesus. In one of my favorite movie trilogies, *The Lord of the Rings*, Frodo in the *Fellowship of the Ring* is at a point where he is weary of bearing the ring. Speaking to the elven queen Galadriel, he says that he wants to give the ring away, and that he does not think he can carry on without his friends. She says to him, "You are a ring bearer, and to be a ring bearer is to be alone." No matter how we want to slice it or dice it, the fact of the matter regarding celibacy is that we are single: solo, alone, unaccompanied.

---

[5] *The Free Dictionary by Farlex, s.v. "character," accessed January 23, 2015,*
http://www.thefreedictionary.com/character.

This aloneness is especially difficult for women because we are relational beings, and we thrive when we have strong relationships around us. We need all types of relationships: family relationships, peer or girlfriend relationships, church and spiritual relationships. However, most of us long specifically for a male romantic relationship. No other relationship can fill this space. We can have great platonic male friends, but they are not the same as boyfriends. I have amazing friends all over the country, and they add much meaning to my life. But at the end of the day *I cannot build my life around these relationships*. When I go to bed at night it is just me, myself and I. If I move out of state or to another city, there is no one else coming along with me.

As women we desire to have a protector and a provider. We also long to be desired and wanted. Now, we know God is our protector and provider, but we want a man who can also play this role in our lives. The fear of being alone becomes even more real when we realize that there are not many single Christian men in most churches. In the singles ministries of many congregations, the women outnumber the men. I recently visited a sister church, and I asked about the singles ministry there. One of the answers was that there were fifty single women and fewer than ten single men, a few of whom were in dating relationships. Those disproportionate numbers can seem staggering, and those odds can lead us to compromise our convictions.

But we cannot give in to our fears. 2 Timothy 3: 6–7 says, "They [godless men] are the kind who worm their way into homes and gain control over gullible women, who are loaded down with sins and are swayed by all kinds of evil desires...." It is interesting that this Scripture says a godless man *worms* his way in; he does not walk right in. This wording seems to indicate that a gullible woman tries to put up some type of resistance, but in the end she lets him in. Why? I cannot speak authoritatively to every situation, but I believe one reason is the fear of being alone. This fear can eat away at a woman's resolve to wait until marriage for unity with another. Sometimes, because we do not want to be by ourselves, we will compromise and take whatever closeness is available to us, rather than hold out for what is better. A gullible woman may think a man will leave her if she refuses to let him into her home.

I have to be honest with myself and with God regarding my fears. I am afraid of the thought of being alone for the rest of my life. I do not want to be a nun; that lifestyle is not what I signed up for. As I have gotten older and the years have gotten longer, being alone forever has started to seem like a real possibility for my life, and I am afraid. But true character is not the absence of feeling afraid; it is the presence of the courage to not back down because of fear.

I have had to confront my fears and address my obsession with marriage and wanting to be in a relationship. My motivation for choosing to live a celibate lifestyle is based on my deep belief that it is right, but for a long time it was not what I wanted. I did not want to be alone, yet I knew that waiting on God was right. I was in misery because I hated the fact that I was alone and single.

I needed to dig deep and figure out what I hated about being alone. The realization I had to come to is that being alone is part of the process of waiting until marriage. Waiting on anything is never easy, but we have to come around to be content with being alone while we wait. It can be compared to the process of having a baby. There is conception, then the development through each trimester, then labor, then the actual birth and even postpartum. Each part of the process is necessary and cannot be avoided. Some women have short labor and some have long, hard, difficult labor; no labor is pleasant, from what I hear, but it cannot be avoided. In the same way, being alone is part of the process of waiting until marriage. How long you have to be alone is uncertain; one woman chooses celibacy and has to wait only a short time to be married, while another may have to wait years before a godly man comes into her life. I had to embrace and accept that being alone was part of the process, and it could not be avoided. It took me many years to finally be at peace with being alone, although, I still struggle with it sometimes!

In the next section, we will delve into the deeper issues that everyone who chooses celibacy must face.

Chapter 8: The Uncertainty of Waiting

We live in a fast food age. We want everything *now*. Society is set up for our convenience and helps us avoid waiting. We can self-checkout, pay for gas at the pump, and pay our bills over the internet, all to avoid waiting in lines. There are even pre-prepared meals available to save us the time it takes to prepare a meal.

This fast-pace mentality shows up in every area of our lives, including our love lives. Those who want to live the single life as God intends, but also have a desire for a romantic relationship, will have to face the hard truth that we must wait on God. If you want to be successful at waiting until marriage, you must not only be prepared to wait but *expect to wait*. There is no getting around it—we have to wait on God's timing to engage in sexual relations. So many want to achieve their life's dream, but do not prepare themselves to wait. This waiting is one of the hardest things about being celibate. Waiting is inconvenient and brings a level of uncertainty with it.

I found that as my years being celibate increased, so did my fears. I started questioning, asking myself, "Am I going to be single for the rest of my life?" Waiting is scary. There are no guarantees and no promises that everyone is going to get married. So many single Christians struggle to maintain longevity in celibacy because they just grow weary. Many of my friends who have quit on celibacy—and thereby on God—got tired and resentful because they did not think it should have taken as long as it did for them to marry. After a certain period of time, they thought that God would surely have blessed them with a mate. Many times we can unconsciously have a set interval that we consider an adequate length of time to be single. We think that because we are obeying God, He will not make us wait too terribly long.

This waiting brings to mind the story of Abraham and Sarah in Genesis 12-21, and of God's promise that they would have a child. God gave Abraham the promise, but it took at least fifteen years, if not longer, before the promise was fulfilled through Isaac. Both Abraham and Sarah were already up in age when God gave the promise. Time was of the essence, yet God had them wait; and at the age of *ninety* Sarah gave birth to a child! I do not know God's reasoning for having them wait so long, outside of maybe proving that nothing is impossible for Him—but they had to wait nonetheless.

But at some point before Isaac was conceived, Sarah grew tired of waiting and took matters into her own hands. She asked Abraham to sleep with her maid, Hagar, so she could build a family through her. Sarah got the child she planned for, but it created more unnecessary heartache and grief for all included, and ultimately she still did not get what she really wanted. What she wanted was a family, but she never saw Hagar's son Ishmael as her own. She referred to Ishmael as "that slave woman's son" (Genesis 21:10). How different would the story have been if Sarah had just waited for God's plan to unfold, instead of trying to speed up the process and create her own solution?

We do not know all that is in the mind of God and His plan for us. We have to walk in faith, knowing that God knows the perfect length of time needed to prepare us for bringing that special person into our lives.

Chapter 9: The Truth about Desires of the Flesh

> Do not think of yourself more highly than you ought, but rather think of yourself with sober judgment, in accordance with the faith God has distributed to each of you (Romans 12:3b).

Being single God's way means no sex until marriage. This reality stumps most single people when they start entertaining the idea of celibacy. For many, the idea of having to cut sex off for an indeterminate amount of time seems preposterous and absolutely impossible. As we have already discussed, God expects and believes that we can be pure and single, and that we can wait until marriage. That would not seem so difficult if we were asexual and had no sexual desires. However, the reality is that we do.

I wish that our bodies had an on/off switch. While we are single we could turn the sex button off, and then when we got married we could turn it on. We do not, however; and so we have these urges and desires for sex but no way to satisfy them before marriage. Many single Christians daily face the struggles of sexual longing, yet feel incapable of truly being victorious in dealing with the desires of the flesh.

Unfortunately, the issue of sexual desires and how to effectively deal with them as a single Christian is not often discussed in the church. As a result, many Christians are naive about their bodies and ultimately underestimate or deny the power of sexual desires. There are three truths that you must understand when it comes to your body:

1. Your body is weak (Matthew 26:40–41).
2. Your body burns with passion (1 Corinthians 7:8–9).
3. Your body has the power to take you over if you do not learn to control it (1 Thessalonians 4:3–5).

These realities can be excruciating to deal with. We live in the world, and sex is constantly around us. Sex is in movies; it is in the music; it is even in commercials. Sometimes the difficulty of celibacy is not just about desiring the act of sex, but craving intimacy with someone we can hold at night.

I see the desires of the flesh being played out in the story of David and Bathsheba in 2 Samuel 11. David was lounging at home when he should have gone out to battle with the rest of the army. Walking

27

around on his roof, he saw a beautiful woman bathing, and inquired about her. He found out that she was the wife of one of his loyal friends, a soldier under his command. Despite knowing this, he proceeded to sleep with her. His sexual desire was ignited by seeing her naked and bathing. Even knowing he should not have done this to a friend, he could not resist. The body is weak, just as Jesus said.

Oftentimes when I have read this passage I have focused on David but not on Bathsheba. Bathsheba was a married woman whose husband, Uriah, was away on business doing what he was supposed to be doing. She apparently came to David without resisting; one thing led to another and before you know it they ended up sleeping together. Why did she cheat on her husband? Why did she not decide to flee and go back home once she realized David's intention? We cannot say for sure, but I can only imagine her feeling lonely, wanting someone to be with her and to hold her. We do not know how long her husband was gone. Maybe she was dissatisfied in her marriage, and the thought of being with the king seemed exciting. Maybe she loved the attention that David was giving her since she was not getting any in her husband's absence. Whatever the reason, she gave in to her sexual desires, and in the end it cost the life of her husband Uriah and that of her newborn child.

Sexual desires are real, and denying them is a real cost we need to count in order to live the single life as God intends. Personally, I am weary of living with women and I am tired of going to bed alone. I want a man in my home and in my bed. This type of raw feeling is not talked about at the women's singles devotionals, but it is reality in dealing with celibacy. It is not easy being pure God's way. But it *is* possible to deal righteously with our sexual desires and wait until marriage to engage in sexual relations.

Chapter 10: Longing Unfulfilled

> "My father," she replied, "you have given your word to the Lord. Do to me just as you promised, now that the Lord has avenged you of your enemies, the Ammonites. But grant me this one request," she said. "Give me two months to roam the hills and weep with my friends, because I will never marry."
>
> "You may go," he said. And he let her go for two months. She and her friends went into the hills and wept because she would never marry. After the two months, she returned to her father, and he did to her as he had vowed. And she was a virgin (Judges 11:36–39).

I am so grateful to God that He put the story of Jephthah's daughter in the Bible. We return to her story here because it validates the thought that many single women have, that not being married is heartbreaking. This young woman could have wept over a lot of things. She could have wept over never fulfilling her lifelong career dream, or not being a mother, or never seeing her family or friends again. Instead she went into the hills for two months to weep over the fact that she would never be married. She chose to spend her last days on earth with friends, weeping that she would die a virgin. Wow!

For years I felt that my desire to be in a relationship and be married was unspiritual. I thought being spiritual meant you were focused on advancing God's Kingdom and were consumed only with that. I felt guilty that the desire of my heart really was to just love God, be married and have a family of my own. I did not have fancy thoughts of ministry or being a missionary. When I would share my heart, I was always counseled to be content and trust God and focus on Him, as if to say I was not already doing that. That counsel always left me feeling like I was doing something wrong.

The story of Jephthah's daughter communicates that it is okay if we feel downhearted because we are single, but we cannot wallow in that sorrow. Despite her sorrow and desire, Jephthah's daughter still honored God and made her life about Him. She did not put God to the side for her desire, but by her sacrifice she demonstrated that her devotion was first of all to Him.

Another woman who has inspired me to trust God with my desires is Hannah in 1 Samuel 1. I *love* Hannah. Her desire for a child was deep and intense. Though her husband tried to counsel her to be grateful for what she had, her heart was not appeased. Proverbs 13:12 is so true: "Hope deferred makes the heart sick." Hannah's desire to be a mother was strong, but she made her life about God—and she got to see God grant her the desire of her heart.

The longing for companionship is just as real and strong as sexual desires. In my opinion, for most women the longing for a mate far overrides the sexual desires. Take Bathsheba, for instance, whose infidelity may have come from a longing for companionship and intimacy in the absence of her husband. Sex was just the means to achieve that.

Longing for companionship is a real cost that you have to count in choosing to live the single life God's way. Like Jephthah's daughter, I have had to continue fighting to make everything about God and serve Him despite my longing going unfulfilled. It is not easy putting God before our desires, and Satan will deceitfully make his way seem a whole lot more tempting and pleasing. God, however, has intended for us to live life and to live it to the full, no matter what our stage in life. To truly be victorious in celibacy, however, we have to face the harsh realities (and joys) of singlehood.

III. Dealing with the Heart of the Matter

Chapter 11: The Quest for Unfailing Love

"What a person desires is unfailing love" Proverbs (19:22a).

Everyone desires unfailing love. It is normal to want love; that is how we were created. Only God can supply unfailing love—a love that is unconditional and will never end. When we do not look to God to meet our need for unfailing love, we start looking for it in all of the wrong places, which is a form of idolatry. How we go about trying to obtain love varies from person to person. Some try to find love and acceptance in food, and some look to a career, success and accomplishment. Others try to find it in a romantic relationship or even through having children.

I was one of those who tried to find love and acceptance through romance. So I started to idolize and focus on men. I did not realize that I was desperately seeking validation and acceptance. Being single and sexually abstinent, I did not see another way to meet my emotional needs.

Since I could never seem to have the real thing—a man—I turned to daydreaming and fantasizing. I was the object of desire. I was pursued. I was fought for. The man would profess his undying love for me. He was everything I wanted and more. He was what every woman wants, but I was the one he chose and came after. For years in my walk with God, I was always confessing such thoughts and trying not to be impure. It took me years, however, to identify that the root issue was not sexual purity but my desire to be loved. I hungered for love and acceptance and was relentless in my pursuit of it. The real issues of my heart were my insecurities, my fears and my longings.

My first year of discipleship was rocky, but I really did not struggle with being single. My struggle began after my first year when I started wanting to be in a relationship. First I just prayed about having a dating relationship. After a few years, though, I started to realize something was wrong. I felt more and more frustrated that God was not answering my prayer for a boyfriend. My sense of unhappiness grew; God was not enough. I started questioning if I had even truly been a disciple because I felt like something was missing in my life. If God was truly the answer, then why did I still feel this unexplainable yearning and longing? I started questioning whether to continue with this celibacy business, and whether I really wanted to walk with God.

After years of misery, I eventually realized that my salvation was at stake, and I wanted to fight for it. If I was going to finish this race and make it to heaven, I had to start dealing with the heart of the matter. I had to admit to myself that I had a deeper problem, and to save my relationship with God I was going to have to deal with my issues and my need for love.

Initially I really did not know where or how to start this process of dealing with my deeper heart issues. At a base level all I knew how to do was pray and cry out to God, so that is what I did. During this time, I came across a Scripture that I started praying for myself:

> [...] And I pray that you, being rooted and established in love, may have power, together with all the Lord's holy people, *to grasp* how wide and long and high and deep is the love of Christ, *and to know this love* that surpasses knowledge—that you may be filled to the measure of all the fullness of God (Ephesians 3:17–19, emphasis added).

What struck me in this passage was that there is a difference between *grasping* the love of Christ and *knowing* it. I also realized that knowing Christ's love is what would fill me and fill the void that I was feeling. When I first studied the Bible I *grasped* an inkling of God's love for me through the Cross, but I really did not *know it* for myself. Many years passed before I realized that what I was missing was knowing God's love—*really* knowing it.

I started praying, "God, help me to grasp your love, but more than that, help me to know it for myself so that I may be filled. Fill my void, satisfy my longing, and help me to be a believer whom you and you alone will complete and satisfy." This was my prayer for years. God helped me to realize that in order to start the process of becoming filled by Him, I was going to need professional help. Sisters had suggested counseling for a long time, but I would dismiss the idea, thinking that praying and studying things out in the Scriptures would suffice. However, when I realized that I was not getting better and that my salvation was in jeopardy, I had to humble out and realize that this was bigger than me. I did not know what I was doing or how to connect it all back to God.

I needed help confronting my past and connecting with how my wounds were manifesting themselves in my pursuit of romance. I needed help confronting my insecurities and self-esteem issues and learning to see myself the way God sees me, turning to Him for validation. Someone had to guide me in learning to get my acceptance, security and love from God.

I needed help handling my fears. I also needed help in learning how to stop worshiping and idolizing men and get my focus and priority back on God. In the following chapters I will discuss each of these in more detail.

I firmly believe that no one can successfully be celibate long-term, much less enjoy it, if the deeper heart issues are not dealt with. I have seen so many sisters pierce themselves with many griefs because they thought they would find solace in the arms of a man rather than in the arms of God. I am so grateful now that God, in His infinite wisdom, knew that I needed to deal with these issues now while I am single; it would be much harder to address them while in the midst of a relationship, making both myself and some poor brother very miserable in the process.

I have seen sisters who chose not to deal with some of these issues before they got married. I saw how their wounds led to heartache, marital unhappiness, and in some cases divorce. A time of celibacy is a great opportunity to work at getting healthy spiritually, emotionally and mentally so that you can really enjoy the life that God wants to give you, and maybe one day even enjoy marriage.

Chapter 12: Confronting Your Past

The purposes of a person's heart are deep waters, but one who has insight draws them out (Proverbs 20:5).

The joys and hurts of our hearts can run very deep; becoming a person of understanding requires digging deep and cutting through all things shallow. Simply put, we must know ourselves truly and fully. Failure to know ourselves can lead to frustration and confusion in our lives.

As I shared earlier, I had to come face to face with issues from my past that had shaped my view of men and relationships. Growing up, I had a lot of deep misconceptions about myself, which led to low self-esteem and constantly seeking validation and love. These weaknesses manifested themselves in my obsession with romance and men. When we avoid facing our past issues and hurts, it can cause us to deal with our emotional needs and our desire for love in unhealthy ways.

These are a few of the questions you may have to ask yourself to start going deep: Who are you really? What makes you tick? What do you really want? What does your heart truly hold dear? What are your desires? Why are you afraid? Why are you the way that you are? Why do you respond the way that you do?

We all have different reasons for wanting to be married, and different things what we hope to gain from a marriage. Some of our reasons may be natural and healthy, and some may be unhealthy. But at the root of all of them is a deeper motivation. I believe that to know ourselves fully, we have to know truly what our motivation is in desiring this intimate relationship.

For you to uncover your deepest motivation for wanting this kind of relationship, you may have to deal with your past. This work is the only way to discover what your patterns are, particularly those you may have had in the world regarding relationships. These revelations will help you not to repeat the same patterns as you faithfully live out your celibacy. We must know ourselves and become people of understanding who can draw out the purposes of our own hearts.

For me, being in a relationship with a man would signify that I was valued and loved, that I meant something to someone, that I was desirable. I simply want to be wanted. I grew up hearing my mom share that my dad really wanted a son and not a daughter. I thought maybe that was why he did not want me and why he did not stay around in my life. I also grew up being teased and called ugly, so I got used to feeling unimportant and unworthy. After I became a Christian, although by that time I understood that I was not physically ugly, I still felt like something had to be wrong with me because I was still single. I wondered if it was my strong personality, or maybe that I was too tall. To me, the men in the church seemed to want a woman who was gentle, soft-spoken and docile, and I always felt insecure because I was none of those things.

As I started the process of dealing with the deeper issues of my heart, I came across the story of Leah in Genesis 29 and 30. Her story resonated with me on many different levels. For the next several chapters I will reference her story in regard to several heart issues.

Leah was the older of two sisters and was probably not very pretty by the world's standards because she had "weak eyes," which basically means she was cross-eyed. The Scriptures describe her sister Rachel as lovely in form and beautiful. Leah probably grew up being told she was unattractive or less than beautiful, and constantly hearing about how beautiful Rachel was. She probably felt the difference all her life.

I remember hearing about how beautiful my older sister was when we were growing up, but no one in my family said that about me. My family even called me ugly a few times. That was very painful. So let us set the stage for Leah. A young stud, Jacob, comes to town; the new guy on the block, he falls in love with a beautiful woman named Rachel and agrees to work seven years to win her hand in marriage. Imagine Leah during this time, secretly hoping that a man will come along who wants to be with her—maybe even fantasizing about Jacob himself. She hopes she will find what Rachel has found. As those seven years go by and no one is in sight, she probably feels a mixture of emotions: sadness, anger, worry, envy, and anxiety about her future.

In those days, women were dependent on men for financial support and security. Being an unmarried woman was shameful and meant an uncertain future. Furthermore, Leah probably felt unwanted and undesirable because of how she looked. After the seven years ended, Leah's father gave her to Jacob in Rachel's place, secretly and deceptively. Thereby Leah's dream came true in part, but her husband was bitterly disappointed in her. In Genesis 29:31 the Bible says, "The Lord saw that Leah was not loved."

Leah was now in an unloving marriage, not of her choice but by her father's decision. I can only imagine the rejection and disappointment she must have felt. I can imagine Leah blaming God and her father for her situation and wondering why this had to be her lot in life. For many of us, bad things may have happened to us in our past, not because of our choices but because of someone else's decision or sin. Some of us may have been molested, raped, physically or verbally abused; we have grown up in dysfunctional families, been belittled and the like.

Neglect, emotional disconnection from parents and absent fathers, or abuse in any form wound us. The scars that remain can leave negative imprints on our hearts, our self-esteem, our psyches, our outlooks on life and our relationships and even our views of God. You may have moved on with your life and chosen to forget about your past, but the hurt and pain will still be buried deep in the recesses of your heart and mind. Certain triggers at different times may bring to the surface what you have been trying to keep buried, forcing you to face what is going on in your heart.

Many of my life patterns and emotional traps came from my childhood, and it was not until I entered counseling that I was able to see them and connect the dots. Many of us exhibit behavior rooted in our childhood. For example, some women who struggle with sexual promiscuity have endured some type of molestation or sexual abuse in their past. Studying the Bible and getting baptized begins the process of healing, but the road to overall wellness can be a long journey. For healing to take place, you have to confront and face the issues of your past.

The process of dealing with the past can be very painful because you may have to relive bad memories. You may not want to deal with the pain of it all; you may choose to ignore it or pretend you are fine, but if you do not bring it up yourself, the past will eventually show up by other means. Not addressing old wounds can have disastrous effects.

One of the saddest stories in the Bible is the account of Tamar in 2 Samuel 13. She was a virgin, a daughter of David, who was raped by her half-brother Amnon. After raping her, he added insult to injury by throwing her out of his house and bolting the door. Scripture says that "Tamar lived in her brother Absalom's house, a desolate woman" (v. 20). How sad! This tragic event stopped her in her tracks; it took her life away. She could not get past the injury of it, and so her brother not only stole her virginity, but she allowed him to also steal her dignity and her future. By not dealing with her past and finding resolution, she was stuck and could not move forward.

God does not want the events of our past to make us desolate or destroy the full life He has for us. We cannot undo the past, but we can come to resolution and peace and discover a full life despite it. Celibacy will be difficult if your search for significance and love leads you in the direction of sex, romance and men.

Some basic, practical steps that helped me confront my past included first acknowledging that I had a problem and realizing I needed counseling. Once I started working on myself, I had to be committed to working issues all the way through to the end. I had to be willing to face the past instead of ignoring it. I put my facade aside and came clean about everything. I also had to be committed to putting into practice the things that the counselor and other spiritual advisers were telling me. I had to learn to deal with the roots of my problems, not just the symptoms. Keeping a journal was helpful at times for me. When it got hard, I had to remember the end goal: to be healthy and to be healed. Ultimately, I had to remember that God was with me, and that I was not alone in this process.

Chapter 13: The Search for Validation and Approval

Continuing with the story of Leah, she was in an unloving marriage. Where was she going to find love now? Should she leave Jacob for another man? Should she pray for Jacob to die, or even kill him so that she could have an opportunity to be with someone else? I can only imagine the insecurities and pain she must have felt every time she saw her husband around Rachel, the way his eyes lit up when he looked at his favored wife, or the fact that he chose to spend his nights with Rachel instead of her. Yes, he would sometimes sleep with Leah but his heart belonged to someone else.

Through the naming of her children, Leah revealed her heart's desires:

Reuben: "Surely my husband will love me now" (Genesis 29:32).

Levi: "Now at last my husband will become attached to me, because I have borne him three sons" (Genesis 29:34).

Zebulun: "This time my husband will treat me with honor, because I have borne him six sons" (Genesis 30:20).

What I see in Leah is a woman who longed to be desired, appreciated and loved. She was searching for validation and approval from Jacob and was hoping that through bearing his kids he would come to love her, treat her with honor and become attached to her. However, despite having his children, she could not win his love, heart or affection. His heart belonged to someone else, and unfortunately nothing was going to change that. As women we can do all kinds of things to try to win someone's love, but love cannot be earned through works, deeds, or gifts—not even the gift of our bodies. I mention Leah because many of us can relate to not being loved or appreciated, and thinking that we can gain love and approval by rushing headlong into a relationship or running after other things.

When I started dealing with my heart issues, I had to come face to face with my low self-esteem, my insecurities, my fears, and my intense longing for love, validation and approval. Like Leah, I was looking for something—rather, someone—tangible to prove my worth and value. I did not feel good about myself and did not think I was special, beautiful or lovable. The longer I was single, the more these feelings were reaffirmed. Brothers and sisters shared how awesome they felt I was and how beautiful I was, but I could not believe it was true. No brothers were pursuing me, dating me or stepping up to claim me.

To me, the proof of my value lay in being in a relationship. Not having a relationship proved the lies I believed about myself. Even though God sees being single as a great thing, a time to be free from concern and to show undivided devotion to Him, I saw being single as a curse. My perspective was skewed because I was looking for a relationship to give me something that only God could provide.

I have seen many women shortchange themselves and God's plan for their lives because they did not trust God and do things His way. Being celibate has brought my issues to the surface and has taught me how to look to God to satisfy my deeper needs. I have also learned my value and worth, and not to settle for just anyone or anything.

Chapter 14: Dealing with the Fear

> Rather, [your beauty] should be that of your inner self, the unfading beauty of a gentle and quiet spirit, which is of great worth in God's sight. For this is the way the holy women of the past who put their hope in God used to adorn themselves [...] You are [Sarah's] daughters if you do what is right and do not give way to fear (1 Peter 3:4–6).

Celibacy exposed my fear. Doing things God's way simply made me afraid. I had to decide whether I was going to do what was right and not give way to my fear. I was deathly terrified at the thought of being single for the rest of my life and never experiencing romantic love, never experiencing companionship, never knowing what it feels like to have someone want and desire me. As each year passed and I grew in age spiritually and physically, my fear grew as well.

Fear is a real, strong emotion. It clouds our judgment. Fear can drive us to be disobedient to God, rash, irrational, angry, combative, violent and idolatrous. Fear steals our joy and our peace. It makes us not do the good we know we ought to. Fear makes us take matters into our own hands rather than trust God to provide what we need and want.

When I hit thirty, it was as if something went off in me. "Oh no, I do not have much time!! The clock is ticking and the countdown has begun." Singlehood for a lifetime started looking more and more like a reality. The multiple unanswered prayers in this area of my life affirmed in my mind that God might have real intentions of keeping me this way.

I did not like the direction I thought God was taking me, and so, like Jonah, I tried to escape and avoid His plan for me. I felt that I could not just sit around and do nothing. I started wanting to compromise, and entertained the idea of going on dates with non-Christian men. I thought about joining non-Christian online dating services—and I did sign up with my church's online dating service. I started traveling and visiting different ministries and going on dates wherever I went. I went to singles' conferences and retreats with the intent of meeting brothers I could go on dates with. It is amazing how you can take spiritual things and make them completely worldly. I was obsessed with escaping singlehood. My fear was leading me to idolatry.

As I exposed and addressed my fear, it revealed my deeper trust issues with God. Did I trust God? Did I trust that He cares about me and my desires? Would He take care of me? Did I trust that God was right and His way was right? Why *should* I trust God? Why did I not trust God? Would God prove faithful?

When I was a child, my desires, my opinions and what I had to say were often overlooked or minimized. My family was extremely frugal and practical so everything we did had to make sense and be reasonable. My desires and wants did not fit into the picture. They were luxuries and not deemed important.

I learned to see God in the same light. What I wanted seemed small and unimportant compared to what He wanted, and whatever He thought was the highest priority. I feared that God did not consider me and my desires in the equation. All that mattered to Him was what He wanted and what He thought was best. I thought that He was a God who withheld blessings and was conditional in the giving of gifts. Trusting God with my love life, something that was very dear to my heart, was scary. Not leaning on my own understanding seemed foolish, and trusting God with all of my heart seemed risky.

As we look back at Leah's story, we read in Genesis 29:31, "When the Lord saw that Leah was not loved, he enabled her to conceive." God saw Leah and her situation. He saw it, and He did something about it. He was aware of her pain and misery. He saw her even though her husband did not.

I have had to dig deep and pray to trust God and believe that He is not oblivious to me. We will look deeper into this later. The point is that I had trust issues that were affecting my enjoyment of life. My fears were crippling me, and I could not move forward until I had addressed them at the core.

Chapter 15: Calling a Spade a Spade: Faithlessness

The journey of digging deep and searching my heart gave me a better understanding of myself and enabled me to begin the process of healing. However, it was very tempting to play the victim and take on a passive mentality. At some point I had to call a spade a spade and admit that a great part of my unhappiness with celibacy came from my faithlessness. I had little faith that God could and would work through me and in my life. My faithlessness had nothing to do with my past or how I was raised, or even my present circumstances. I had to face and acknowledge that I had *chosen* to be faithless rather than to be faithful.

Faithlessness can kill the enjoyment of living. Hebrews 11:1 says, "Now faith is confidence in what we hope for and assurance about what we do not see." Somewhere along the line, I stopped feeling confident and assured that God had an incredible plan for my life. I stopped believing that God would work things out for my dreams to be fulfilled. I stopped believing that God's way made sense, and that it actually works. For many of us, as the time spent waiting for our desires to be fulfilled increases, our faith decreases. Maybe you started out having great faith that God wanted to use you to do amazing things in His church and to give you life to the full, but as the years have passed by you have allowed your faith to slowly dwindle.

Faithlessness is the kryptonite of hope; it will kill hope quickly. Faithlessness can present itself in many forms. We may not always be able to identify it as what it is. To keep our hopes and dreams alive, we have to be aware of faithlessness, and how it can manifest itself in our lives.

Faithlessness sometimes starts out as a feeling of frustration, which can lead to us trying to take matters into our own hands. This desire is a big issue for many people. We love to be in control and try to manipulate situations to make things work out as we think best. Remember Amnon, whom we spoke of earlier. Why did he rape Tamar? "Amnon became so obsessed with his sister Tamar that he made himself ill. She was a virgin, and *it seemed impossible for him* to do anything to her." (2 Sam 13: 2, emphasis added). The situation seemed impossible to him. So instead of taking it to God and letting God work it out, he tried to speed up the process and make it happen himself. Now, most of us probably have not gone to the extremes of excessive force like Amnon, but like him, many of us start to feel that our situations are impossible. Instead of trusting God, we try to take control. We scheme and plot to make someone fall for us, or maybe we start going out on dates with men in the world, reasoning, "I cannot sit around and do nothing." Or we start making compromises to suit ourselves. Whatever the case, we have got to examine our hearts and our actions. Is faithlessness the motivation for our actions?

Some may argue, "Does this mean that I should do absolutely nothing when I see an opportunity?" Others may say, "Ruth did not sit back and do nothing; she took action." The litmus test to expose our motivations is found in 1 Peter 3:1–6:

> Wives, in the same way submit yourselves to your own husbands so that, if any of them do not believe the word, they may be won over without words by the behavior of their wives, when they see the purity and reverence of your lives. Your beauty should not come from outward adornment, such as elaborate hairstyles and the wearing of gold jewelry or fine clothes. Rather, it should be that of your inner self, the unfading beauty of a gentle and quiet spirit, which is of great worth in God's sight. For this is the way the holy women of the past who put their hope in God used to adorn themselves. They submitted themselves to their own husbands, like Sarah, who obeyed Abraham and called him her lord. You are her daughters if you do what is right and do not give way to fear.

The key is being submissive to God by doing what is right. Our spirits should be gentle and quiet because our hope is in God. An unbelieving man can be won over for God when he *sees,* not hears about, the purity and reverence of another's life. Peter says, "Do not give way to fear." Many times the temptation to take matters into our hands comes because we are afraid that if we do not *do something* we are going to miss out or have a less-than-favorable outcome. Amnon's spirit was frustrated because his hope was not in God. In the case of Ruth, she did not take matters into her own hands; she obeyed the instruction of the older woman God had placed in her life, and went and lay down at Boaz's feet. She did what was right by her obedience. Maybe you want to take matters into your hands by dating an unbeliever. Such a compromise is faithless on your part. Standing firm in your convictions and doing what is right is the faithful decision.

Another way faithlessness manifests itself is through depression. Before I go into this, I know that there are many people who have clinical depression and other forms of mental and emotional illness, and that is another matter entirely. What I am addressing is an intense sadness that is triggered by circumstances. Hannah, tormented and provoked by her rival, would weep and not eat year after year when her family would go to worship and sacrifice to the Lord. The key here is the continual sadness caused by her circumstances and how it interrupted her life, especially her worship of God.

Faithlessness will interrupt our worship, rob us of our quality of life, and stop us dead in our tracks spiritually and emotionally. I remember so many times crying uncontrollably whenever I went to a wedding, watched romance movies or even spent time around my married friends. It got to the point where I wanted to avoid married people completely.

Hannah was in an extremely difficult and sensitive situation. It is unreasonable to think she would never feel sadness or be downhearted about it. Any suffering causes sadness, and even Jesus was sorrowful and troubled in the Garden of Gethsemane (Matthew 26:36–46). Yet He *did not stay* in a state of sorrow, and neither can we. Hannah, despite the process taking so many years, finally got it. She got real and open with God about her misery, her great anguish and her grief. After her heartfelt prayer, it says in 1 Samuel 1:18–19, "Then she went her way and ate something, and her face was no longer downcast. Early the next morning they arose and worshiped before the Lord and then went back to their home at Ramah." Once Hannah dealt with her faithlessness, she was able to go on her way, go on with her life and worship God.

Sadness has become the barometer of my faith. Usually I am sad when I start looking at the reality of my situation and feeling hopeless. Like Hannah, I have to turn to God and be real. Most times I walk away feeling hopeful and no longer downcast.

Depression is one of those issues which can make it hard for sufferers to face the fact that they have a serious problem. In no way do I want to minimize or downplay the seriousness of mental or emotional illness. Sometimes it is much more than just a faithlessness issue. Depression should be taken seriously when it starts interfering with the quality of your life and your relationships. Part of Hannah's recovery was her dealing with the deep matters of her heart. She got gut-level honest with herself and God, and she turned to the only One who could help her. For many, though, professional counseling and medication are additional God-given tools that can help them gain mental and emotional health.

Faithlessness is one of those deeper issues of the heart that we have to confront to be truly victorious in living the celibate life. Take inventory of your heart, and do not ignore what is really going on. Be brave and be ready to call things what they are. Now that we have addressed the deep things of the heart, let us look at how we can embrace the journey!

IV. Embracing the Journey

Chapter 16: The Cross Is Our Salvation

Celibacy, with all of its various facets, is rewarding when we decide to embrace it. We can never truly appreciate this stage of our lives while we are in it if we do not choose to look at it through heaven's eyes. It is often said that hindsight is 20/20. Once married, many then realize how valuable, special and amazing being single truly is. Many wish that they had done more, lived more, gone after their dreams, and better appreciated their time as singles. Facing the realities of being single and dealing with the heart of the matter now, while we are in it, helps us discover how to truly get the most out of this time. Let us live out our celibacy in such a way that we do not have to look back with regret on our single lives.

Once I started facing the deeper issues regarding celibacy, I needed help finding my way out of the maze of my heart. I needed to learn how to embrace and enjoy the journey as God wanted me to. First I had to become convinced that Jesus and the Cross are my salvation in every way. I then had to learn to be committed to becoming and staying emotionally healthy. Doing that work meant learning to embrace the pain, which meant I had to find gratitude in the midst of my situation. Lastly, I had to learn to get my priorities right and put my focus back on God!

Everyone desires unfailing love. That is what Proverbs 19:22, mentioned in Chapter 11, tells us. We can search for unfailing love in many places, but God is the only source. Even though I had grasped God's love for me to some extent when I first studied the Bible, I had never truly come to know it for myself. Christ's love did not compel me because I was not truly convinced that He had died for me and only me. I had to get beyond the knowledge that He died for the world, and accept that He died for *me* because He loved *me*!

I have come to realize that I need a lot of reassurance. I believe God knows that we all long for proof of love. In every relationship we have, no matter the type, we want to be assured of the other person's love, affection and loyalty. We not only want proof of love; we want proof of our value, of our worth and significance.

Whether single or married, all of us must come to a conviction that our value and worth is found only in the Cross and that only through the Cross do we find proof of God's unfailing love for us! Even a husband or wife can never be unfailing in their love. Isaiah 43 says:

But now, this is what the Lord says—

he who created you, Jacob,

he who formed you, Israel:

"Do not fear, for I have redeemed you;

I have summoned you by name; you are mine [...]

For I am the Lord your God,

the Holy One of Israel, your Savior [...]

Since you are precious and honored in my sight,

and because I love you,

I will give people in exchange for you,

nations in exchange for your life.

Do not be afraid, for I am with you [...]" (Isaiah 43:1–5).

These are not just nice, fluffy words. God demonstrated this type of love for me at the Cross. He gave Jesus for my ransom. He gave Jesus in my stead. Since I am precious and honored in His sight, He gave Jesus' life in exchange for my life.

The reality that God had redeemed me and summoned me *by name* was something I had always wanted but never experienced before in my life. God wanted *me*! He claimed *me*! He chose *me*! The part where He declares "You are mine" proves He wants *me*. In every historical romance novel I had read before I was a Christian, the man always said, "You are mine." It was not an afterthought. It was not, "Oh, let me choose her because she is so pathetic." God desired and wanted me! God wanted to be with me so badly that He would go to any length, give up anything and everything He had to win me over and win me back. I imagine God saying, "I have got to have her. No matter what." He was willing to give Jesus in exchange for me because I was precious and honored in His eyes.

The Cross also proves to me that God loves me just the way I am. Romans 5:6–8 says:

You see, at just the right time, when we were still powerless, Christ died for the ungodly. Very rarely will anyone die for a righteous person, though for a good person someone might possibly dare to die. But God demonstrates his own love for us in this: While we were still sinners, Christ died for us.

46

When God chose me I was powerless, ungodly, a sinner. I was neither at my best nor looked my best. God chose me when I was at my worst, yet He still saw me as precious and honored and decided to rescue me. I did not have to jump through hoops or change who I was to win His love and affection. See, I was fearfully and wonderfully made (Psalm 139:14) and God knew that full well, even if I did not. I did not have to be ashamed. I did not have to hide. He loved me then and He loves me now, point blank, period.

The Cross will always be my proof that I am loved and that I am valuable. That fact can never be changed or taken away. A husband can leave me or die, but the Cross stands forever. I so wanted proof that my life had meaning and value, and that is why I craved validation, acceptance and love. The Cross gave me that proof, and still does. Jesus felt I was worth being spit in the face for; that I was worth being flogged and crucified for; that my life was worth saving; that my life was worth His carrying His cross so that I could be His. Jesus is the knight in shining armor who came and saved the damsel in distress: ME! One of the best Bible studies I ever did was when I looked at God as a husband:

You will be a crown of splendor in the Lord's hand,

a royal diadem in the hand of your God.

No longer will they call you Deserted,

or name your land Desolate.

But you will be called Hephzibah,

and your land Beulah;

for the Lord will take delight in you,

and your land will be married.

As a young man marries a young woman,

so will your Builder marry you;

as a bridegroom rejoices over his bride,

so will your God rejoice over you (Isaiah 62:3–5).

The thought that God takes delight in me, no matter how I mess up, is amazing! God rejoices over me; I am like a crown of splendor in His hand. He adores me: insecure, prideful, selfish, unloving me. *To be able to put marriage in its proper place in our lives, we must understand that we are*

47

already loved and valued. Whatever your past and whatever you are going through right now, look at yourself the way God looks at you. I have to constantly fix my eyes on the Cross whenever I am feeling insecure, ugly, unworthy or the like. The Cross will forever be proof of my value and worth as a woman and as a human being. It can never be taken away. That is the Good News of the gospel!

Chapter 17: Becoming Emotionally Healthy

Fascinatingly, celibacy exposed my emotional dysfunction and the bad habits connected to it. I had never really made emotional health a priority because I never saw how it affected my life and my relationship with God. But many of the teachings in God's word are designed to help us learn how to be emotionally healthy and balanced.

I realized eventually that I could not be spiritually healthy if I were emotionally unhealthy. As I started understanding God's love for me and the reality that He loves me for who I am—the good, the bad and the ugly—it gave me the courage to not only face, but to decide to change the bad and ugly parts of myself. I quickly realized that if I was going to be committed to emotional wellness and ultimately to being faithful to God to the end, I had to learn how to start addressing and dealing with the feelings in my heart on a consistent basis. God's love gave me the courage to start being completely open and transparent about those hard things with Him, myself and those around me.

Throughout the Scriptures, different writers get gut-level honest with God. We see the writers in Psalms, Jeremiah and Lamentations all express their discontent and misery. Being faithful to God's plan of celibacy and emotional wellness requires getting to this place of complete transparency. The hardships and the struggles that come with this way of life will most certainly hit, but complete openness is the way to being victorious over them.

Complete transparency is a small but essential part of being emotionally and spiritually healthy. It requires trust, humility and courage, which have to be learned. All of us come from different backgrounds and deal with our emotions in different ways. How we handle conflict, how we deal with our hurts, pain and disappointments, and how we express those things all indicate the condition of our emotional health. Stuffing the pain inside, ignoring it, sweeping it under the rug, pretending it does not exist, minimizing the issue, justifying, fits of rage, or medicating the pain are all emotionally and spiritually unhealthy. Honest prayer and openness with other people are the alternatives.

Maybe you feel bad or guilty at the thought of being totally open and honest with God. You might think it is not right to question God, to express discontent, to get angry with Him. But the examples in the Bible suggest that honesty is what God wants. The entire book of Habakkuk is about a prophet questioning God and looking for answers—which God provides! Job also works through his bitterness, anger and pain with God. At the end of the book of Job, God again responds to man's pain. Anger, hurt, pain, disappointments, sadness and despair are all human emotions. Our goal should be to deal with them in a spiritual and healthy way.

I grew up in an extremely private home. Everything that happened in the house stayed in the house. We never discussed with others outside the home what was really going on. We never even completely told each other everything, especially our feelings. I did not have a problem with being open, but as I grew up I was frequently chastised for "talking too much." When I had conflicts with others, I handled the situations by losing my temper and putting my adversaries in their place. When I could not verbalize my anger, I learned to deal with my pain, my insecurities and my need for love through daydreaming and fantasizing.

When I became a Christian, I knew that blowing up at people was wrong, so I learned to stuff my feelings and artificially "overlook offenses." Unfortunately, unmanaged emotions would build up inside of me until I would eventually go off on someone over the littlest thing. I did not know how to resolve conflict or deal with my emotions in a godly and righteous way.

Over time, as I started trying to be more honest with God about how I was feeling, I dealt with God much the same way I dealt with people. I would have a tirade toward God in my prayers. I would fling my Bible. I was extremely rude and disrespectful with Him, but I did get all my emotions out. Then I would feel fearful because I did not know how He was going to respond. I thought He might strike me down for my disrespect.

To my surprise, instead of being struck down by God, I discovered an intimacy with Him that met my soul's needs. I saw Him answer me through the Scriptures and through my time with Him, much like He did with Job and Habakkuk. I learned to be brutally honest with God because I discovered that He was my safe place, my refuge, my shelter from the storm.

God can handle whatever I throw at Him. He is slow to anger and not reactionary. He deals with me lovingly but firmly. When I get angry with God, I tell Him. When I am disappointed with God, I tell Him. Whatever I am feeling, I tell Him. He continues to answer me through the Scriptures. I truly believe this process has saved my life and has kept me in this journey as long as I have been.

I have seen many friends walk away from God because they could not take the celibate lifestyle anymore. In every case, I discovered that they had not been truly honest with God and others in the early stages of their struggles. They kept it all locked away inside and continued

50

living the spiritual facade. Eventually they looked up and decided they wanted out.

Learning how to handle your emotions can be a journey. As I have mentioned, my journey to getting emotional health—which in turn meant getting spiritually healthy—required professional counseling. Not everyone may need professional counseling as I did, but I do believe everyone needs "one another" relationships to be emotionally healthy. You cannot make this journey alone. You need others to help you and hold you accountable, but you also need those who you know will listen to you, love you and tell you the truth in a safe, non-threatening atmosphere. Two great books that I recommend for learning how to deal with our emotions are *Emotionally Healthy Spirituality* by Peter Scazzero and *Secure in Heart* by Robin Weidner.

A Bible study on how Jesus dealt with His emotions also helped me tremendously to be committed to emotional wellness. It taught me how to deal righteously with my desires, as well as the emotions that came along with them. Matthew 26:36–46 tells the account of Jesus in the Garden of Gethsemane. In verse 37 it states that when Jesus was with His three friends, "he began to be sorrowful and troubled." Jesus felt emotions. Being sorrowful and troubled is okay. I can so relate to Jesus because as a woman, there are times when out of the blue I can begin to feel emotional. I may see a couple together, hear a love song on the radio, or start thinking about how long I have been on this journey, and before I know it I begin to feel overwhelmed just as Jesus did. But while *having* emotions is not sin, how I choose to *deal* with those emotions can be.

Jesus was open about His emotions. It says in Matthew 26:38, "Then he said to them, 'My soul is overwhelmed with sorrow to the point of death. Stay here and keep watch with me.'" He was speaking to Peter and the two sons of Zebedee. Jesus was a grown man, their Teacher, Lord and leader. The temptation could have been, "I have to be strong for my men. I have to hold it together. I cannot let them see me weak or vulnerable. If I lose it as their leader, who will lead them?" Jesus, however, chose the route of humility and honesty. He told them quite frankly that He was overwhelmed with sorrow and needed them to stay and keep watch with Him. I have been sad, but I have never been as sad as Jesus describes Himself here: overwhelmed with sorrow to the point of death. No other emotion to feel but sorrow: sorrow to the point He felt like dying. Jesus understands the dark depths of depression. At a time when it could have been tempting to want to be alone and work His emotions out privately, Jesus asked His friends to stay and keep watch with Him.

Jesus was also honest with God in His prayer: "My Father, if it is possible, may this cup be taken from me." (v. 39). He told God exactly what He wanted. He did not sugarcoat it or beat around the bush. In His prayer, He surrendered and deferred to God: "Yet not as I will, but as you will." Surrender does not mean faithlessness. In verse 53, right before Jesus was arrested, He said, "Do you think I cannot call on my Father, and he will at once put at my disposal more than twelve legions of angels?" Jesus had complete and absolute faith that God could and would grant what He asked. He chose, however, to wrestle His desires out with God and submit to Him.

Lastly, Jesus taught me that sometimes the road to resolve and surrender is not a one-time prayer. It may take multiple prayers in our garden to gain resolve in our emotions. When Jesus left the Garden of Gethsemane, He was resolved and no longer sorrowful and troubled.

Jesus' example has become my pattern for dealing with my emotions and learning how to stay committed to emotional wellness. I have in no way mastered my emotions, but I can say I have learned to make emotional wellness a priority in my life and my journey with God. I have come to discover that Jesus' way is the best way to face and deal with the emotions that come in this journey of celibacy. Doing it His way has helped me learn better how to enjoy the journey.

Chapter 18: Embracing the Pain

Unfulfilled desires are painful. Being single and celibate can be very difficult for those who long for companionship, romance, and having a family. We see Jephthah's daughter weeping for two months over never getting married. We see Hannah year after year bitter in soul, weeping and not comforted because she could not become a mother. One of my objectives in this book is to validate that the pain is real. However, I do not want to just validate the pain, but help us to see things from God's perspective and to truly find the full life that He has intended for us.

No matter what your heart desires, you will have to go through the desert before you reach the Promised Land. During the Exodus, God gave the Israelites promises of deliverance; He assured them that He would bring them to the Promised Land and that He would take care of them, love them and be faithful to them. God provided great miracles and signs when He brought them out of Egypt. What the Israelites did not realize was that the road to the Promised Land was not going to be easy. They had to go through the desert, where they experienced hunger, thirst, heat, insects and scorpions.

In Deuteronomy 8 it says that God humbled the Israelites, causing them to hunger. Then He fed them with food from heaven to teach them that "man does not live on bread alone but on every word that comes from the mouth the Lord" (v. 3). In other words, the desert was God's teaching tool for the Israelites. God, in the middle of the desert, did great wonders to provide for them. Water came from rocks. Manna came down from heaven. God was preparing them, teaching them to rely on Him (Exodus 16–17). Yet when they came to the borders of the Promised Land they had not realized that they were going to have to fight to win the land. God had promised that He would give it to them, but they were going to have to work for it by facing giants. That generation, however, chose to not believe God or trust in His deliverance, and in their unbelief they rebelled against Him. God ultimately told that generation of Israelites that they would all die in the desert and would not enter the land that had been promised (Numbers 13–14).

The desert was not a punishment, but a training ground to prepare the Israelites to enter the Promised Land and enjoy its benefits. They had to hunger and thirst so that they would learn to rely on God when things got difficult and when they had to face their enemies. Although the first generation died, after forty years in the desert the next generation was fully prepared to take what was promised to them, as we see in the book of Joshua.

God has used celibacy to refine my character like nothing else. It has been God's training ground to teach me how to rely on Him, trust in Him and believe in Him. He has used it to teach me how to fight and work for my salvation with fear and trembling, to make me healthy and whole emotionally, mentally and spiritually. Ultimately, He has used it to build my character and help me become more like Jesus.

For a long time, I despised my celibate life because I did not look at it the way God looked at it:

[...] "My son, do not make light of the Lord's discipline,

and do not lose heart when he rebukes you,

because the Lord disciplines the one he loves,

and he chastens everyone he accepts as his son."

Endure hardship as discipline; God is treating you as his children (Hebrews 12:5–7).

All hardship is discipline from God. He is using the struggles and the pain to teach you what you need to learn and to prepare you for something great. God Himself acknowledges that the discipline is painful. I had to learn to embrace the pain and not see it as God not loving me, wanting to hurt me, or wanting to withhold from me. Through the pain, I had to learn to choose to believe God and trust Him. I had to choose to believe that somehow or another this was good, even though it did not feel good. I learned that believing God is a choice just as unbelief is a choice.

I do believe as well that celibacy is a training ground to prepare us for something great like marriage. The Bible says that those who marry will face many troubles (1 Corinthians 7:28). That is a sobering reality of getting married. Every married person I talk to, whether Christian or not, says the same thing: marriage takes work. If marriage were easy there would not be so many divorces.

A great marriage takes a lot of work, humility, prayer, and tears. Who is to say that God has not used celibacy to prepare me to become a great wife? My relationship with God has taught me how to fight to make a relationship work. It has taught me submission and trust, even when I do not know the plans and cannot see the way out of difficulties. It has taught me patience and waiting on God and His timing *and* about denying myself and putting His will before my own. I have also learned about honesty, openness and not avoiding conflict. God has taught me that He is my source for joy, comfort and unconditional love. Will I not need all these things in my future relationship with my husband? Maybe the hardships I am facing now as a single person are equipping me to face the troubles and hardships that will surely come in marriage. And if I do not ever get married, maybe the hardships I am facing are preparing me for some other great thing God has in store for me!

God's goal in every situation is to build our characters and get us to become more like Jesus, to save us and save others in the process, and ultimately to get us all to heaven. Remember that heaven, not marriage, is truly the Promised Land. God will use every stage in our lives, including celibacy, to help us reach the *real* Promised Land.

Embrace the pain of the journey, knowing in your heart that as parents discipline their children, so God disciplines us. Do not resist the pain, fight the pain, ignore the pain or try to fix it yourself. Allow the hardship and the pain of celibacy to mold you, knowing that God disciplines us for our good. He knows that later on it will produce a harvest of righteousness and peace for those who have been trained by it (Hebrews 12: 11).

Chapter 19: Embracing the Wait

Choosing not to give way to fears about singlehood means choosing to embrace waiting on God to fulfill the desires of your heart. The uncertainty of waiting is one of the realities of celibacy. It was one thing to accept that I had to wait, but it was another thing entirely to embrace it. The word *wait* is mentioned 129 times in the Bible. There is something about waiting that God wants us to get. Embracing the wait ultimately means embracing God's will, surrendering to it and putting our trust in Him. It leads to peace.

You may be familiar with Jeremiah 29:11 where God says, "For I know the plans I have for you," followed by a promise full of hope. But do you know why God gave the Israelites this promise? These Israelites had been sent into exile into the land of Babylon because they persisted in sin, despite God's many warnings to them through His prophets. In Jeremiah 28, a false prophet named Hananiah came to the exiles in Babylon, claiming that God had told him to tell the people that in two years God would deliver them from the hand of the Babylonians and send them back to Jerusalem, the capital of their homeland. In response to this false claim, God sent a message to the exiles via Jeremiah, letting them know that He was going to deliver them in *seventy* years, not two. Yikes! Seventy years is an extremely long time to wait to be delivered.

These two chapters of Jeremiah contain a wealth of valuable lessons that we as singles can learn about how to embrace the wait. God does not want us to wait in vain. There is a reason and a plan for everything that He does. The first step to embracing the wait is to understand that God determines our circumstances.

In Jeremiah 29:4, it says *God* caused them to be sent into exile. We must be convinced in our hearts that God has either allowed or caused every situation that we are in. Psalm 16:5 (NIV 1984) says that God assigns us our portion and our cup. 1 Corinthians 7:17 states that each person should retain the place in life that the Lord has assigned to them and to which He has called them. God assigns us our place in life. I have prayed to God that Romans 12:2 would be my absolute conviction: that God's will is good, pleasing and perfect.

God determines whether we remain single or get married, and He determines how long we will be single. For many years as a Christian, I did everything within my power to change my circumstances, yet I was still single. I finally had to realize that maybe I was fighting against God and His will for me. I believe very strongly that God will grant me the desire of my heart, but I finally had to accept that my desire must be according to God's will and not my own. I had to trust that God's will and timing is good, pleasing and perfect.

The next step in embracing the wait is accepting that God desires for us to grow and thrive in our current situations while we wait. God told Jeremiah that in seventy years He was going to come back and fulfill His promise to return His people to Jerusalem. What did God intend for them to do while they waited for His deliverance? Sit around and do nothing? No! He gave them very specific instructions: build houses, plant gardens, get married, have children and marry their children off. God instructed them not to put their lives on hold.

Choosing to live your life to the full means choosing to make the most of your present circumstances while you wait for God to make your dream a reality. God wants us to bloom where He plants us! God did not want the Israelites to put their lives on hold while they waited for the distant future, but to enjoy their present by investing in their today. So many of us put our lives on hold waiting until marriage. If you dream of buying a house when you are married, then why not buy a house now while you are single? If you imagine traveling the world when you get married, then travel now while you are single. God does not want us to put off living our lives while we wait for Him to work. As singles, we have the fewest restrictions on our time. *Now* is the time to do the things you would love to do; *now* is the time to enjoy your life.

Choosing to live your life while waiting also embodies blooming emotionally, mentally and spiritually in your present situation. Take this time to discover who you really are, what you genuinely like and dislike. Take this time to grow in your character, in godliness and holiness. Learn to be the best you—the you that God wants you to be—today.

To embrace God's will we also must make peace with our present circumstances. The Israelites were forced from their homeland and deposited into a foreign country. Human reaction would be to hate Babylon and to wish its demise. God, however, told them to "seek the peace and prosperity" of Babylon and to pray for it (Jeremiah 29:7). Peace is freedom from disturbance, war, hostilities, tumult or commotion. If we want to be single with character as we dream of marriage, we must seek internal peace and acceptance of our current place in life. To seek something means you do not have it; we have to actively go after peace, and pray for the prosperity of our current situations.

One of the things that I have done to help myself have peace with being alone is to thank God in my prayers for being single. How many of us thank God with a sincere heart for this? The Bible says "Rejoice always, pray continually, give thanks in all circumstances; for this is God's will for you in Christ Jesus" (1 Thessalonians 5:16–18). Since I started lifting up prayers of thanksgiving, I have seen God bless me with the peace that transcends all understanding (Philippians 4:47).

Now, do not get me wrong; I still have frequent moments when I question and wonder why I am single, and feel sad because of it. That is why God says to *seek* peace and pray for it. It does not come naturally, and it requires consistency. There are days when I am faithful and at peace with my circumstances, and days when I am not; on those days I have to fight in prayer to be at peace. The key is to not allow ourselves to remain in discontent and emotional turmoil. We must make peace in order to stay faithful through the wait. We must come to peace with being alone.

Finally, to embrace the wait we have got to let go of false dreams and hopes that can hinder our acceptance of God's will. There were false prophets among the Israelites, and God said not to listen to their dreams. Just like the Israelites, we can be deceived. False dreams and hopes make us feel good—they are what we want to hear and believe; many of us even encourage them. Modern false prophecies and deceitful dreams can come from many different places, including within ourselves. Society, modern culture, and even family and friends can be false prophets telling us what we want to hear. See if you recognize any of these false messages:

1. Being alone is not okay.

2. You deserve to have someone in your life, and God will understand if you compromise your convictions.

4. You do not have to be so intense and hardcore about giving up sex.

5. You will never get married and will die an old maid if you do not take matters into your own hands.

6. God wants you to be happy, and whatever makes you happy is fine.

7. You must be married by a certain time, or have children by a certain time.

8. Time is ticking away and you must take action before it is too late.

9. You know a man in the world loves you and it can work out even if you do not do it God's way.

How did the people know that Hananiah was a false prophet and Jeremiah was true? How can you distinguish between false hopes and true dreams? False hopes are contrary to what God commands. They also generate sinful tendencies, particularly idleness and a sense of entitlement. God does not want us waiting in vain, nor does He want us to think that it is all about us. Remember what God told the Israelites to do: build houses and settle down. If they had believed the false dream of God delivering them in two years, why would they build houses and plant gardens? Who would spend that time and effort, only to leave it in two years? If they had not invested in their current circumstances, they probably would have been idle and felt entitled because they thought they deserved better. False dreams and hopes make us put our lives on hold and not invest in our todays.

We must beware of false prophets and our own false dreams so that we can fully accept and be surrendered to God's plan for our life. You can tell when false dreams and hopes are pulling you away from God because you see their effects:

1. Idleness, inactivity and waiting in vain

2. Lack of investment of self, time and resources

3. Divisions, hostilities, complaining and discontentment

4. Short-term focus on life, instead of long-term focus on eternal life

5. Pursuit of ungodly things and defiance of God's commands

The ability to embrace the wait comes from a deep trust that God has a plan for your life and that He knows what He is doing. As I think about the Israelites' seventy years of captivity and when the time had finally come for them to enter the new chapter of their life, returning to Jerusalem, I imagine that they were able to see that the wait was not in vain. They were entering this new chapter with everything they had gained during that seventy-year period. They could look back with a sense of accomplishment, not regret. In addition, they had great joy in anticipating what God was going to do in this new phase of their lives! Do not just accept that you have to wait, but embrace the wait and make the most you can of this time!

Chapter 20: Finding Gratitude

Gratitude, in any language or culture, is a beautiful thing. We all feel inspired when we see people who, despite the odds against them, defy those odds and choose to be grateful in the process. Gratitude is heart-warming and empowering. It brings peace and joy. It makes life fun and makes us radiant! Being around those who are ungrateful is burdensome, depressing and draining. When I see singles who are grateful for their relationship with God and their single lives, it makes me feel that I too can conquer the world and can do anything with God.

Looking back at Leah and her story in Genesis, a beautiful thing that stands out in her life is that she chose gratitude. Her grateful heart shows in the naming of some of her children:

Judah: "This time I will praise the Lord" (Genesis 29:35).

Gad: "What good fortune!" (Genesis 30:11).

Asher: "How happy I am! The women will call me happy" (Genesis 30:13).

In such a heart-wrenching situation, she demonstrated that we should live by the motto, "If life gives you lemons, make lemonade." Her situation was not her choice, was not what she dreamed about or desired, but this was her life. Leah chose to find the good in her circumstances and be grateful.

Embracing the journey of celibacy and enjoying it will empower us as we fight to be grateful in our circumstances. Scripture says, "Give thanks in ALL circumstances, for this is God's will for you in Christ Jesus" (1 Thessalonians 5:18). Giving thanks may seem challenging in unpleasant circumstances, but it is so vital because it unlocks the door to peace.

There is so much to be grateful for in being celibate! We have this time to be free from concern, to pursue our dreams and become great for God. We have the flexibility and freedom to go where we want and to choose to use that freedom to serve God and others. We get this time to grow and have our characters refined without the complication of being in a marital partnership. We have freedom in every way! Not only do we have all this, but our salvation awaits us in heaven. We have forgiveness of sins, the Holy Spirit within us and Jesus sitting at God's right hand interceding for us. We have the truth and we know the way!

Being grateful has to be very deliberate. It is a decision, not a feeling. As I shared in the last chapter, I had to learn to pray pointed and specific prayers of only thanksgiving. When I felt like complaining and grumbling about the singles ministry, the lack of brothers, my life, the church, why I was not going on dates, why I was not in a dating relationship, why I was still single after many years, my pain and my struggles, I had to learn to nip that in the bud by focusing on the positives. Philippians 4:8 says, "Finally, brothers and sisters, whatever is true, whatever is noble, whatever is right, whatever is pure, whatever is lovely, whatever is admirable—if anything is excellent or praiseworthy—think about such things." I have learned not only to take my frustrations to God, but to change my perspective and my mood by being grateful.

In Lamentations Jeremiah states that he remembered his affliction and bitterness, and it made his soul downcast, but when he called to mind the promise of God, it gave him hope. What we are thinking about affects our moods. When our souls and emotions are in a dark place, what we call to mind can make a world of difference.

There is more than one way to become grateful. One tool that has helped me call to mind positive things is my personal book of remembrance—a gratitude journal. I have written down all of my answered prayers and the miracles God has done in my life. When I am in a low place, just reading through it encourages me and leads me to gratitude for God. At other times, singing songs of praise and thanks has led me to gratitude even when the last thing I wanted to do was sing. Other ways to focus on gratitude include making a list of different people or things to be grateful for, writing thank-you cards, reflecting on those less fortunate or in worse situations, watching *The Passion of the Christ*, and keeping a box of notecards with God's promises nearby so that you can pull them out and read them in moments of stress or despair.

Embracing and enjoying the journey with celibacy will come as you make deliberate decisions to be grateful and to give thanks in the midst of it all. The grass always seems greener on the other side, but if you water right where you are planted, you will start to see that your grass is already green with God.

Chapter 21: Living by Faith

"For we live by faith, not by sight" (2 Corinthians 5:7).

      Celibacy for God is about living by faith and not by sight. Faith is the fuel that enables us to live this life and persevere in it. It is extremely important to our relationship with God and to our salvation. When I went to an online concordance and typed in the word *faith*, there were 458 references to it in the Bible. We are saved by grace through faith, and faith keeps us saved. Abraham was declared righteous because he believed God. Faith is what heals us. It unlocks God's power. When Jesus was in His hometown, He was not able to do much there because of their lack of faith (Matthew 13:53-58).

      I mentioned earlier some of the ways faithlessness can manifest itself. The reality is that without faith we have lost the battle. We cannot live this life of celibacy without it. Faith is what keeps us going. It is what makes miracles happen. It is what keeps us walking on water, not sinking and drowning.

      Satan knows how precious and important is our faith, and it is the one thing he is always striving to steal and destroy. He knows if he can take our faith from us, he has won. Without faith we cannot please God or even be connected to Him (Hebrews 11:6). In living a life of discipleship and submission to Jesus' lordship, the battle always comes down to whether we will choose to believe what we see and can understand, or whether we will choose to believe what God says. For many of us, going merely by sight, our singles ministries seem like barren wastelands when it comes to finding prospects for marriage. Women in particular can feel that finding a man who loves God, has godly character, has a successful career and is emotionally and spiritually compatible with them is like trying to find a needle in a haystack.

      We must choose to walk by faith on a daily basis. The way is truly narrow, and not many find it or stay on it. Faith is what keeps our feet on the narrow road. In learning how to walk by faith, I went to the man who is described as the father of faith: Abraham. It says in Romans 4:

> Against all hope, Abraham in hope believed and so became the father of many nations, just as it had been said to him, "So shall your offspring be." Without weakening in his faith, he faced the fact that his body was as good as dead—since he was about a hundred years old—and that Sarah's womb was

also dead. Yet he did not waver through unbelief regarding the promise of God, but was strengthened in his faith and gave glory to God, being fully persuaded that God had power to do what he had promised. This is why "it was credited to him as righteousness" (Romans 4:18–22).

Abraham had faith in a seemingly hopeless situation because he faced the facts, was fully persuaded of God's power and held on to the promise of God.

It may sound contradictory, but being willing to face the facts is the first step towards walking by faith. Being faithful is not about being deceived, living in a make-believe world or placing our hopes on a fantasy. It certainly is not about pretending that the truth of the matter does not exist. Faith acknowledges the seriousness of the situation and the realities involved. Being realistic does not equate to faithlessness. God does not want hype or pumped-up egos. True faith stares the situation in the face and believes in a mighty God despite the facts. Abraham admitted to himself that he was one hundred years old and that his wife, Sarah, was ninety years old. It cannot get any more impossible than that. True faith starts with awareness of the reality of the situation.

Despite the facts, Abraham was *fully persuaded* that God is able. He believed that God has the power to do anything. He believed that nothing is too hard for God or impossible for Him. We serve a God who is able to do immeasurably more than all we can ask or imagine (Ephesians 3:20). God has the power to do what He has promised, no matter your circumstances. Nothing is too difficult for the Lord!

In choosing to walk by faith, we must realize that our sight will show us many things that will seem big, overwhelming and too powerful for us. Our sight will show us that we are vulnerable, weak and do not have the strength. If our eyes are focused only on ourselves, it will discourage us. Instead, we must fix our eyes on God and remember who He is. He is the one who spoke into the darkness and created light. He is the one who by His power, wisdom and understanding created all that we see. He is the one who raised Jesus from the grave! Our God is able, and like Abraham, we must be fully persuaded of that fact.

To keep walking in faith, consider keeping a journal of answered prayers and victories that you know the Lord has brought. Turn to it when your faith starts to waver. Another great faith builder is studying out different stories in the Old Testament. In these stories we see God deliver His people from even the most difficult circumstances. Listen to accounts of other people's victories. Keep inspirational stories in your heart to give you hope. Find and read books on the promises of God, and study out the promises that encourage your spirit. Another great remedy for shaky faith is doing an in-depth study on the nature of God.

Like Abraham, we must be fully persuaded about God's nature. I encourage you to study out God's power, His grace and love, His strength, His faithfulness. The Bible tells us:

Keep your lives free from the love of money and be content with what you have, because God has said,

"Never will I leave you;
never will I forsake you."

So we say with confidence,

"The Lord is my helper; I will not be afraid.
What can mere mortals do to me?" (Hebrews 13:5–6).

We must be content because God promises that He will never leave us or forsake us, and we can rely on His faithfulness. Walking by faith is what celibacy is all about. Never forget God's promise to be with us. Never stop believing that He has power, and that He is faithful.

Chapter 22: Prioritizing and Focusing on God: Recap

Embracing, enjoying, and appreciating celibacy came to me once I learned that God had to be the object of my focus, my affection, my devotion and my love. Being a disciple of Jesus is not about me simply having a great life and enjoying the fellowship of believers; it is about loving God and discovering that He is my reward, my prize, my treasure, my crown and my life. Like the Bible says, "Whom have I in heaven but you? And earth has nothing I desire besides you" (Psalm 73:25). The end goal of life is getting to be with God. I cannot wait to be with Him and to talk to Him face to face in heaven! Fighting this fight, living this life, is not about having a great marriage but about having God.

It took me a long time to learn this focus regarding celibacy, and for this lesson I am very grateful to God. As I shared earlier, because of my search and need for love I was obsessed with romance and men. I looked to them instead of to God and found only heartache, pain and confusion. I truly believe that had God given me a boyfriend and husband early in my discipleship, that brother would have become my focus and my god. I would have been unhappy because I would have looked to a man to fulfill a need that only God could fill. Celibacy exposed the sin of idolatry in my heart. I have to consistently face the fact that idolatry is a part of my sinful nature, and if I am not careful I can easily start looking to other things besides God for comfort and love.

I was obsessed with marriage, romance and men before I was a disciple, and for years in my walk as a disciple. Obsession is a misguided and misplaced priority that comes from a skewed perspective of need. My perspective of what I needed was off, and that led me to locate the desire for marriage in an improper and unrealistic place in my life and then to worship it.

In *The Silence of the Lambs*, there is a part where the psychopath Hannibal is in his prison cell and Clarisse, the heroine, secretly visits him to get his help in a serial murder case. She is desperately trying to get Hannibal to tell her who the killer is. He does not give in to her pleas but rather tries to get her to find the answer herself. He does this by asking her questions. Two of his questions really struck me and made me think about myself: "What is his (the killer's) nature?" and "*What need does he serve* by killing?"

When I think about what I do, I have to ask, what is my need? My actions and priorities reveal who I am and what I think of as important and necessary to meet my needs. When I was obsessing over relationships, my need was for acceptance and unfailing love; I longed to be validated and wanted. I thought this need would be satisfied in a relationship, so I pursued that perceived solution and went after it. I chased it with all my being. When I could not have an actual live person, I tried to meet the need by daydreaming and fantasizing. I learned to escape in my mind, and I created all kinds of elaborate love stories to satisfy my need.

In Romans it says that true transformation starts with a renewed mind (Romans 12:2). I had to straighten out my perspective of what I needed. In order to do that, I first had to realize and believe that I already had everything I needed through my relationship with God.

In Luke 10:38-42 Jesus told Martha, who was distracted, worried and upset about many things (can you relate?), that only one thing is needed. According to Jesus, this was being with the Lord and focusing on Him; that is what Mary was praised for. As a single woman who longed to be married, I had to accept that only one thing is needed in every situation: being with the Lord and listening to what He says.

Martha was troubled and upset even though the Son of God was in her home. Being a good hostess was her top priority. That role became more important than listening to what Jesus had to say. She wanted to serve Jesus (and that was noble and good), but somewhere along the line she lost sight of what was truly valuable.

For a long time, I felt I needed to be in a dating relationship and heading toward marriage to feel good about myself. Like Martha, I would get distracted, worried and upset about all the details of the who, how, where, when of getting married. Like Martha, I lost sight of what was truly needed, and my priorities got jumbled up. 2 Peter 1:3 states that we have all we need for life and godliness through God's divine power. Do you believe and know that you already have what you need for life right now as a single woman?

I used to feel I needed a man in my life to validate my existence and confirm my worth. I believed a man would finally prove that I was not abnormal. This "need" distracted me, worried me, upset my spirit for years and drove me to fixate on having a dating relationship. I had to learn that my true need was already met at the Cross. I had to become content with the Cross being the only validation I required. If I needed a husband in my life right now, then God would have provided it.

Problems in our spiritual lives come because we confuse wants with needs. A need is something essential for life. A want is not essential; it is a perk, a benefit, a desire. When we place a want on the same level as a need in our minds, it becomes a high priority. Then every thought and action focuses on achieving and fulfilling that want. For many single women, the problem comes when we feel we need a romantic relationship in order to be content and happy. I had to understand that I did not *need* a relationship, I *wanted* a relationship. Having a man in my life was not essential for me to live my life to the full. What I needed was God and His love.

I had to learn to refocus and reset my priorities. First, I had to acknowledge that I had a problem and that my focus was off. Second, I had to deal with the root of my problems: my insecurities and my hunger for love and acceptance. I did that with the help of professional counseling along with spiritual counseling, reading many books and studying God's word to readjust my thinking, and staying in prayer. Third, I had to retrain myself day by day, sometimes moment by moment, to set my focus back on Jesus. Martha started out with good and noble intentions to serve the Lord. In the process of doing that, she lost sight of what was truly important—what she most needed. I had to learn not to give way to fear by choosing instead to trust God, focus on Jesus and be obedient to Him.

Again, I do not want to give the illusion that I am "cured" in any way. I still talk a lot about my single status; I am writing a whole book about it, for pity's sake! It still dominates my conversations, my thoughts and my prayer times. I have learned that putting the focus back on God and making Him my priority is a deliberate and intentional action that I must take on a daily basis. I have been able to identify that when I am feeling troubled, upset, worried and bothered in my spirit, it is usually because I have taken my eyes off God and am looking to the wrong things. I have learned that whenever I get my eyes and my heart back on God, the joy comes in and the peace begins.

Please consider everything presented in this section about embracing and enjoying the journey of celibacy, and take time to really reflect on where you currently are in your life. Now that we have looked at facing the deeper issues and embracing the journey, we are ready to look at living a life of purpose!

V. Living Life to the Full

Chapter 23: God's Purpose for You

> The thief comes only to steal and kill and destroy; I have come that they may have life, and have it to the full (John 10:10).

When I think of my life before having God, I realize that I had no life, really. I was empty, afraid, lonely, miserable, and powerless to fight the sin in my life. I wanted to be different but I did not know how. I wanted to live an amazing life, but I did not know the way or who could help me find it.

Then someone sat down with me and shared the good news about Jesus. Jesus was the good shepherd who cared that I was lost, confused, and going to hell. He was the shepherd who left the ninety-nine other sheep to come look for me and find me. He was the only one who could make me new and give me eternal life—the only one who could give my life purpose.

I realized then that I needed this Jesus and all He had to offer. I wasted no time and left everything I had to follow Him and make Him my Lord. When I was baptized, I remember how glad I was to have God in my life. Nothing else mattered. I was right with God and wanted only to live for Him and do His will.

Yet, as time passed, I grew older spiritually and physically and got caught up with the matters of this world. My gratitude for God was replaced with discontent, resentment and bitterness. I was mad at God because He was not allowing my life to unfold the way I had envisioned. Disillusioned, I wondered why I did not have the Christian dream timeline: get baptized, leave the campus ministry, get a job, get married and start a family. Trying to understand why God was keeping me single, I wondered which sin was I being punished for or what godly attribute I lacked.

I stayed in the wilderness of discontent for a long, long time. When I moved from Chattanooga to Atlanta in 2005, I was weak in my faith and barely holding on. I joined a church of about fifty people who banded together to make a difference. Nine years later, that church of fifty had grown to almost 500 in attendance on Sundays. I saw a powerful God work in a powerful way. My faith was not only restored but was expanded. I saw our singles ministry convert and baptize a great number of single men and women. I came to see and know what it looked like to be a part of a dynamic singles ministry that was growing and having an impact. Singles had an important role in the church and my personal contribution mattered, as it still does.

During this time, I not only discovered my purpose, but also, more importantly, how to live my life to the full. In John 10:10, Jesus states that He came to give us life. That refers to eternal life, but I believe it also includes living a life to the full even now while we are here on this earth. When I was unhappy, I had to make a choice: stay discontent and bitter, or discover my purpose and live a full life. Many people today live life with no clear idea of what their purpose actually is. Even as Christians, many of us are very unclear about what God wants from our lives and how He wants to use us. I do not profess to begin to know what God's clear purpose is for your life, but I do know that there is one.

God has a purpose for you right now! No matter your relationship status, your situation or circumstance, God has a plan for you right now! For many years, I mistakenly believed that my life would only really begin once I got married. I felt that as a single woman I did not have an important role in the church. And of course I just could not wait to get married; I wanted to leave singlehood so badly. But I have learned to savor and enjoy each moment as a single, and believe that God has something great for me right now. Now—while you are single—is the time to discover what God's purpose is for you, not later.

Proverbs 16:3 says, "Commit to the Lord whatever you do, and he will establish your plans." God wants us to have plans that we can commit to Him. Discovering your unique purpose will take prayer, Bible study and planning. If you are not sure where to start, a good place to begin is taking inventory of your strengths, abilities and talents. After that, take inventory of your heart's dreams and desires, and figure out your passions as well. From there, come up with ideas on how you can make these things become reality. Do not think about the reasons why they cannot or will not be possible. A great perspective to take is, "If money, time or resources were not an issue, what would I want to do now?" Whatever the answer, let that be a starting guideline. God can take care of all the issues, so start researching, get some advice, make a plan, and commit it to the Lord.

Be open-minded as you are searching for your purpose in celibacy. Many of us will discover our purpose through disappointment, pain, suffering and trials. I speak from experience on this. I used to be a woman without a dream or a purpose, but God has taken my weakness and my pain and has done something with them I never could have dreamed of. He made me an author and a public speaker—things I did not even know I could do. Do not let discouragements or failures stop you; God may choose these very things to use to glorify Himself through you!

While you discover your unique purpose, know that God has a general purpose for you as a disciple as well. God desires that every disciple be focused on accomplishing the task that He has assigned us: making disciples and spreading the gospel. No matter what phase of life we are in, this task will never change. God wants us to use the gifts He has given us to make the gospel attractive and to edify or build up the church (Matthew 28; Romans 12; 1 Corinthians 12).

In the book of Haggai, God rebuked the Israelites because each person was focused on building his own house and pursuing his own agenda while God's house was in ruins. God does want you to pursue your dreams and make your house great, but He wants you to make sure that His house, the church, is taken care of first. In Matthew 6, Jesus commands us to seek *first* His kingdom and His righteousness. Are you as busy doing the Lord's work as you are with pursuing your personal dreams? Have you neglected the Lord's work to complete your own? God's task has not changed. He still wants us to work the field and take care of it. Jesus compares the lost to a harvest. He needs workers to go into the field and bring in the harvest (Matthew 9:38, Luke 10:2). Once we bring the harvest in, we have to take care of it. There is much to do, so we have to constantly keep our focus on making sure we are doing the Lord's work.

A purpose God has for every daughter of His is to learn to become a woman of noble character. In my pursuit of marriage, I started studying out that topic and praying that God would prepare me to be a godly wife. In that study, I was led to Proverbs 31, which is titled "The Wife of Noble Character." I have looked at the Proverbs 31 woman many times. I used to feel inadequate and overwhelmed by all of her accomplishments. The description of her can be daunting, even a bit overwhelming, because she seems like Super Woman. She was a wife, a mother, a manager over the servant girls, and a businesswoman. She is described as a hard worker, hospitable, physically strong, early riser, fashion designer, and philanthropist. She never dropped the ball; everything was accounted for and in place. However, what was it about this woman that really made her so incredible? It was not just her list of accomplishments.

I recently discovered that the Proverbs 31 woman had *character*, which was reflected in the things that she did. All of her accomplishments came as a result of her character. Too often I think we can miss the point of Proverbs 31, as I had, by focusing on what she *did* rather than who she *was*. Her noble character came from her fear of the Lord. Because of her relationship with God she was able to be the woman that she was and do the amazing things that she did. She did not achieve these things by her own strength and ability, but by her fear of the Lord. The passage says that a woman of noble character stood out as rare, so I decided to find a woman in the Bible who was unmarried and had noble character. I was led to Ruth.

In Ruth 3:11 Boaz tells Ruth, "All of my fellow townsmen know that you are a woman of noble character." Ruth was single and yet was known among all the men for having a noble character. I have prayed in the past to have a Ruth-and-Boaz relationship but I never prayed to *be* a Ruth—to have her character. What are some attributes of noble women of character? Here are some of the parallels I see between the Proverbs 31 woman and Ruth:

The Proverbs 31 Woman	Ruth
Feared the Lord	Feared the Lord
Trustworthy and reliable	
Consistent	Consistent
Decision maker and eager to work	Asked to go work; self-starter
Willing to go the distance to provide for others	Went to a new country for Naomi
Business-smart, with her own earnings	Provided for Naomi
Not physically weak/a hard worker	Worked steadily in the fields
Willing to stay up late	
Able to laugh at the days to come	
Welcomed the poor and met their needs	
Planned ahead to meet future needs	Stored food for Naomi
Creative with her home	
Supplier of a commodity	

As I reflect back on my journey with God, I see Him using celibacy to shape my character. I was like an onion, and God tenderly but firmly peeled away many layers to refine me. Being a woman of noble character is a lifelong pursuit, but one of the great benefits during your time as a single woman is being able to work on yourself. God will shape our characters to refine us for our unique purpose. It takes character to pursue your purpose and make it a reality.

Working on your character while you are single also helps you to be the best *you* that you can be before you add another person into the equation with marriage. As I think back on it, I am glad God has kept me single. I had so many issues to work through that I know for sure I would have made a mess of marriage. A great marriage starts with being a great single woman. Are you able to provide for yourself, much less provide for others? Are you ready to be a partner, willing to go the distance for someone else? I do not think anyone ever "arrives" at character perfection, but now is the time to prepare yourself to be the greatest woman for God that you can be.

Chapter 24: Choosing a Life of Purpose

I hope by this time you have discovered that there are a few consistent themes in this book, one being that we have the power and ability to make decisions. Living a life of purpose starts with a choice. We have to *decide* to live a life of purpose exactly where we are. It is not going to just happen. At some point you have to choose to go after what you want and not allow anything to deter you. There are three aspects of this choice I want to examine here: You will have to decide to not eat the bread of idleness, commit to being persistent, and make the most of your opportunities.

Idleness – There is an old saying that goes, "Idle hands are the devil's workshop." Idleness breeds nothing good and will destroy your purpose. Some of the definitions of idleness include "not working or active," "habitually doing nothing or avoiding work," "lazy," and "frivolous."[6] A woman of noble character does not eat the bread of idleness. We can get a deeper understanding of how destructive idleness can be when Paul writes to Timothy concerning younger widows (women who were single):

> Besides, they get into the habit of being idle and going about from house to house. And not only do they become idlers, but also busybodies who talk nonsense, saying things they ought not to. So I counsel younger widows to marry, to have children, to manage their homes and to give the enemy no opportunity for slander. Some have in fact already turned away to follow Satan (1 Timothy 5:13–14).

This Scripture talks about single women getting into the habit of being idle, of doing nothing, being inactive and lazy. It is easy for single women, especially women without children, to get into this habit. This period of our lives is when we have both the most time and possibly the most money because we have the fewest responsibilities. Many of us have gotten into the habit of going to work and going home and watching TV. Celibacy is difficult to maintain happily if we are women who are in the habit of being idle.

---

[6] *Dictionary.com*, s.v. "idleness," accessed January 23, 2015, http://dictionary.reference.com/browse/idleness.

What types of people do the Scriptures tell us are prone to idleness, and do you resemble any of them? Some are gossips; if you do not have any business of your own, you spend your time concerned about what other people are up to. But if you have a full life and a full schedule, what time would you have to sit around and talk about other people's business? Some are busybodies; you meddle in other people's lives. If you have your own purposeful agenda, you are not so concerned about other people's issues. Some idle women say things they ought not say, and eventually they do things they ought not do. One of my biggest weaknesses when I am idle is daydreaming and fantasizing, an activity that takes up much time. I struggle with this because by nature I am lazy.

Paul counseled the younger widows to get a life by getting married and having children. Fortunately, we live in a day and age where getting married is not our only option, but I feel the counsel is still the same: get a life. Get yourself involved in things that will keep you active, and prevent you from getting into the habit of doing nothing. Mental inactivity breeds sinful tendencies like daydreaming, fantasizing and impure thoughts. Inactivity breeds overindulgence and feeds addictions. I have noticed that when I am at home doing nothing, I find myself wanting to eat all the time. Note that this advice is not a license to overwork yourself. The key here is to not get into the *habit* of being idle.

Persistence – In Luke 18, Jesus shared the parable of the persistent widow to show us that we should not give up. Persistence requires character; this means not allowing failure, defeats, obstacles, sin, weakness or anything else to stop you from going after what you want. In this parable the persistent widow was rejected and refused multiple times, but she kept asking. One of the great things about being celibate is the freedom to pursue your dreams without fear of adversely affecting anyone except yourself. Once marriage and children come into the picture, you may not be able to freely pursue your dreams, because you have to make sure to provide for the needs of a spouse and perhaps children. Do not be deterred; keep going after whatever dream God has laid on your heart. The encouraging part of the parable is that the widow eventually got what she wanted. There is hope with God!

Not giving up means being consistent in prayer. Jacob was a fighter and had a fighter's mentality when he wrestled with God over the desires of his heart in Genesis 32. He refused to let go until he saw his request granted. Many of us get discouraged and lose faith when God does not answer our prayers the way we want or when we want, so we stop asking and believing. I find it interesting when I speak to sisters who express a desire to be in a dating relationship and get married, yet are not praying about it. Even though God has yet to answer my prayer for a mate, I have resolved to keep praying about it, despite times of discouragement, until God answers. Be persistent in prayer!

Opportunities – When we choose to live a life of purpose, we have to be willing to create some opportunities and be ready to seize opportunities when they present themselves. Peter seized the opportunity of a lifetime when he saw Jesus walking on water and asked to come out and walk toward Him. To this day Peter is the only man who could say he walked on water! Do not sit around waiting for something to happen. Do what you can and make something happen right where you are.

If nothing else, use your time now to set yourself up so your dream can become a reality. Be on the lookout for the opportunities that will appear. Once I put a dream to be able to speak at a conference into my impossible prayer box. I prayed about it over the years. One day I happened to see on Disciples Today a request for elevaTED speakers to share a video talking about a subject. I seized the opportunity. I had to come up with an idea and determine what my points would be, and then I had to find someone to film me and send it out for me. God did the rest! God cannot work if we do not put ourselves in a position to be blessed.

Dream about having a great life for today—for right now. Dream for your life, for your immediate circumstances as well as your future. Do you have six-month, one-year, five-year and ten-year goals? Pray that God will reveal to you your unique purpose right now as a single. My prayer is to have no regrets when I walk into marriage. I want to feel like I have accomplished many of my dreams, and that I can look back at my single days with joy in my heart.

Chapter 25: Putting on the Spiritual Armor of God

To live my life to the full, I had to start working on resolving the issues of my past in my heart, and then start building godly character. Remember from Chapter 7, character is defined as having moral strength and integrity. Moral strength means having the power and the courage to take a stand for your beliefs, even if no one else around you does. Moral strength also means not giving in to the temptations that every person faces. We build character by putting on the full armor of God. Ephesians tells us:

> Finally, be strong in the Lord and in his mighty power. Put on the full armor of God, so that you can take your stand against the devil's schemes. For our struggle is not against flesh and blood, but against the rulers, against the authorities, against the powers of this dark world and against the spiritual forces of evil in the heavenly realms. Therefore, put on the full armor of God, so that when the day of evil comes, you may be able to stand your ground, and after you have done everything, to stand. Stand firm then, with the belt of truth buckled around your waist, with the breastplate of righteousness in place, and with your feet fitted with the readiness that comes from the gospel of peace. In addition to all this, take up the shield of faith, with which you can extinguish all the flaming arrows of the evil one. Take the helmet of salvation and the sword of the Spirit, which is the word of God.
>
> And pray in the Spirit on all occasions with all kinds of prayers and requests. With this in mind, be alert and always keep on praying for all the Lord's people (Ephesians 6:10–18).

Living for Jesus is a spiritual battle in which our enemy is not flesh and blood. For singles living celibately, many days of evil will come our way, so in order to be strong we must put on the full armor of God every day. Will you be defeated, or will you still be standing after all is said and done?

The Bible gives some insight into the characteristics of women who lack moral strength. 2 Timothy 3:6 says, "[Godless men] are the kind who worm their way into homes and gain control over gullible women, who are loaded down with sins and are swayed by all kinds of evil desires."

How does a man *worm* his way into a woman's home and gain control of her? The woman has to let him in. As we saw in the chapter on flying solo, so many women fall for the smooth talk and sweet nothings that men whisper into their ears. A gullible, weak-willed woman is someone who is accustomed to giving in. She has not trained herself in consistently putting on the full armor of God and therefore has left herself vulnerable to attack.

It takes moral strength to say no to ungodliness and be adamant about what is right. A man cannot worm his way in if there are no cracks in your resolve or weak areas in your stance. A woman of character has control over herself. She is not easily swayed by her desires, but rather has the strength to deny herself.

You build moral strength every time you say *no* to your desires and *yes* to what is right. The more you do this, the stronger your resolve will be. This development may seem difficult, but everyone can build character and grow in moral strength. How do we, as celibate singles, put on the full armor of God? There are several pieces of armor that we must learn to wear: truth, righteousness, the readiness that comes from peace, faith, salvation and the word of God. Let us look practically at how to live this way on a daily basis.

The Belt of Truth

In the struggle to live a celibate lifestyle, the first piece of armor we must live in daily is truth, or honesty. Honesty is the key that helps us to continue walking in the light:

> This is the message we have heard from him and declare to you: God is light; in him there is no darkness at all. If we claim to have fellowship with him and yet walk in the darkness, we lie and do not live out the truth. But if we walk in the light, as he is in the light, we have fellowship with one another, and the blood of Jesus, his Son, purifies us from all sin (1 John 1:57).

How do we live by the truth? By not living double lives, otherwise known as hypocrisy, and by confessing our sins. "Therefore confess your sins to each other and pray for each other so that you may be healed. The prayer of a righteous person is powerful and effective" (James 5:16). We have to constantly stay open with other spiritual people about our temptations, our sins, our fears, our desires and everything about our lives. If you claim to be celibate but are secretly involved in impurity, you lie and do not live by the truth. Maybe you think, "Well, I am not having sex, so I am okay," but you are involved in other forms of impurity like masturbation, pornography, fantasizing and daydreaming. It will be only a matter of time before you want the real thing. Be committed to staying open and confessing your sin daily.

The Breastplate of Righteousness

"Do not love the world or anything in the world" (1 John 2:15). Righteousness is a key piece of armor in the celibate lifestyle. It is the breastplate that protects our hearts in the battle. Being righteous is simply doing what is right, having a commitment to not simply hear the Word but do what it says. To live a celibate lifestyle, we need deep convictions about personal righteousness. Often it can be easy to do righteous things in the presence of others, either for praise or from fear of being held accountable if we do otherwise. At some point you have to decide that you do what you do because you do not want to sin against God. You have to realize that ultimately it is He who will hold you accountable on the last day. How is your personal righteousness?

The Readiness that Comes from the Gospel of Peace

Peace allows us to be ready. As we discussed earlier, a huge part of celibacy is waiting, and that requires a lot of patience and peace. Being at peace helps us complete our course, running the race for God. Remember, God is not hurried. He has a plan.

Readiness and peace go hand in hand. Readiness is being prepared, quick, willing and positioned to fight. Lack of peace makes us unprepared, dull, slow, unwilling, inept and useless. In Luke 21:34, Jesus says that the worries of life distract us from the reality that He is coming back. Worry and anxiety weigh the heart down like steel-toed boots weigh a runner down. That is why it is important to stay open about your worries, fears, and anxieties. In the battle of living the celibate lifestyle, we have to fight daily to be at peace with God's timing and His plan for us. We also stay engaged in the battle by sharing the gospel of peace to those who do not have it. Maintaining an outward focus on seeking and saving the lost will equip us to be prepared and engaged in the spiritual battle.

The Helmet of Salvation

In fighting the good fight for celibacy, your mind must be set on the prize: salvation awaits you in heaven. The goal of celibacy is to prepare us not just to enter into a great marriage, but to enter something far greater: heaven. Our thoughts and sights must be set on our destination.

Satan wants us to be shortsighted and think only about our immediate wants and desires, living only for this life. Just as a helmet protects your head, remembering your salvation protects you from the lies of the devil. Jesus said that Satan is the father of all lies and that when he lies he speaks his native tongue (John 8:44). Satan will make sin look very tempting and pleasing, filling our heads with all kinds of falsehoods about God and our worth and value. He wants us to abandon God and, ultimately, our salvation and our place in heaven.

The realities of living our single life God's way will produce struggles, difficulties and pain. God, however, promises that there is a reward for doing what is right. During those times when I was tempted to date non-Christian men or when I felt like being single was too much to bear, God would grant me moments of clarity when I would think, "Is this worth leaving God for? Is it worth losing my salvation over?" Then I would remember my days before I became a Christian. I remembered the loneliness I felt. I remembered the fear I felt because I knew I was separated from God. I remembered the anguish and despair I felt about my life when I was by myself: life was meaningless and everything was a chasing after the wind. I remembered the sin I hated and was enslaved to. Remembering my past helped me to stay the godly course.

Despite the hardships in my journey of the last twenty years with God and celibacy, God has allowed me to put on the helmet of salvation, and I remember my name is written in heaven in the Book of Life (Revelation 3:5). I remember that this world is perishing and that I have a better home to look forward to. I remember that I am an alien and a foreigner in this place, but my citizenship is in heaven (Ephesians 2:19). I remember that the Bible says there will be no marriages in heaven (Matthew 22:30). I remember that in all things God works for the good of those who love Him (Romans 8:28). I remember who I am: a daughter of the King (1 John 3:1). I remember that I am part of a royal priesthood, a chosen people, a holy nation, a people belonging to God (1 Peter 2:9). I remember, above all, that neither trouble nor hardship nor persecution can separate me from the love of Christ, and that in all these things I am more than a conqueror through Him who loved me (Romans 8:35, 37).

The Shield of Faith

Faith is described as a shield. It is what we use to ward off the flaming arrows of the evil one. Shields come in many different shapes and sizes. There were shields that, when set upright, would hide the warrior's whole body when he crouched low behind it. Then there were the round shields that we typically see in movies, that cover only the mid-torso area. In the spiritual battle the size of our shields is determined by the size of our faith.

Shields are moveable objects. Unlike a helmet which stays put on our head, or a breastplate which stays fastened to our chest, a shield is meant to move. It is not meant to stay in one place. Whatever direction the arrow comes from, a shield has to move to meet and ward off that arrow. Our faith is meant to expand and grow. Our faith will be tested in many different trials and hardships, and no matter what the trial is, our faith has to meet that demand.

There are times in the battle when we can get stuck in our faith. Discouragement, doubt, fear, worry, anxiety: these are some of the flaming arrows that Satan throws at us. If our shield of faith is not able to ward off these arrows, then our faith can become paralyzed.

Is your faith growing? Faith is a choice, not a feeling. Faith has to be deliberate and intentional and has to be put to work, just like a shield has to be used in warfare. Our faith is not going to magically grow and expand on its own. We grow by adding to our faith and feeding it daily. In 2 Peter 1 it says:

Make every effort to add to your faith **goodness; and to goodness, knowledge; and to knowledge, self-control; and to self-control, perseverance; and to perseverance, godliness; and to godliness, brotherly kindness; and to brotherly kindness, love. For if you possess these qualities in increasing measure, they will keep you from being ineffective and unproductive in your knowledge of our Lord Jesus Christ (v. 5–8, emphasis added).**

Make every effort to add to your faith, in increasing measure, the qualities mentioned above. The promise is that if we are adding to our faith then it will keep us from being stuck, or in other words, ineffective and unproductive.

Romans 10:17 says, "Consequently, faith comes from hearing the message, and the message is heard through the word about Christ." There is no other way to feed our faith and help it grow other than being in the word of Christ, the Bible. Are you growing in your Bible study? The size of your faith will be ultimately determined by the time you spend in Bible study. Are you reading your Bible every day? Examining the Scriptures daily as the Bereans did (Acts 17:11) will make us grow in our faith. You cannot expect to have faith without being in the Word daily. Do not make excuses. You make time for whatever you want to do, and for whatever you deem important. Have your shield of faith in place to help you to be victorious in the spiritual battle.

The Sword of the Spirit

The Word of God is compared to a sword. Every great samurai has a great sword and knows how to use it effectively. Every Christian has access to an amazing and incredible sword. No person's sword is better than the others; we all have the same sword, one with divine power to demolish strongholds. The sword is the only piece of the armor that is not only defensive but offensive as well. We protect ourselves with the sword, and with it we can cut the enemy down. With our sword we can tear down Satan's strongholds, Satan's arguments and every pretension that Satan puts up (1 Corinthians 10:4–5). How amazing! We are not powerless when we have our sword in our hand. We can defeat the devil.

It has been said that practice makes perfect. Growing in effectiveness in using your sword takes reading it daily and putting it into practice daily. In children's classes we teach a simple but profound song that says, read your Bible, pray every day and you grow, grow, grow. As basic as it seems, many Christians find it a huge struggle to simply read their Bibles and pray every day. In John 15 Jesus tells us that if we remain in Him, the vine, and His words remain in us we will bear fruit; apart from Him we can do nothing. Often we underestimate and minimize the impact of not being in God's Word daily. Successfully living a life of celibacy requires that we remain in the vine. Our strength comes from staying in the Word, handling it correctly and living it out.

In Matthew 4, Jesus shows us a great example of how He used the sword of the Spirit in the spiritual battle. He was led into the desert by the Holy Spirit and after forty days of fasting He was vulnerable physically, emotionally and mentally. Satan saw this as an opportune time to attack. Jesus, however, fought off the devil and his temptations by using the word of God. It was obvious that the Word was written on His heart, because He was able to quickly use it to cut down Satan's attacks. Are you growing in your knowledge of the Scriptures? Are you still memorizing Scriptures, writing them on your heart the way you did when you started the race? Have you studied the Scriptures in the areas of Satan's strongholds in your life, in order to demolish them? Have you grown to where you can use the Scriptures to teach others and lead non-believers to Christ?

In the battle for living celibacy every day, we have to put on each article of the armor and take up our sword daily, learning to become deft in its use. Armor is useless for protection if we do not put it on. Realize that the power to be victorious and to defeat Satan lies not only within our grasp but is actually in our hands!

Chapter 26: The Impact of Prayer

And pray in the Spirit on all occasions with all kinds of prayers and requests. With this in mind, be alert and always keep on praying for all the Lord's people (Ephesians 6:18).

After Paul describes the armor of God in Ephesians 6:10–17, he talks about prayer. If you get nothing else from this book, I hope you get this message: you will not have a powerful and impactful life for God unless you have a powerful and impactful prayer life. Without prayer, everything else we have looked at is pretty useless. Those who live life to the full live a life full of prayer.

People stand in amazement when I tell them that I have been celibate for twenty years. My perseverance in living this life has only been possible because of prayer. Recently a sister shared with me that in a Bible study on Jesus' lordship with a single friend, they were discussing the issue of having to be celibate as an unmarried disciple of Jesus. She mentioned me and how long I have been celibate. Her friend studying the Bible (someone I know as well) exclaimed, "She always seems so happy, like she is enjoying her life!" I was encouraged; it made me marvel at how much God has changed me and my life. But I want everyone to know that there is absolutely no way that statement about me could have been true without many prayers to God.

I cannot even begin to recount the many nights of tears and prayer; the endless hours I have had to pour out my heart to God in bitterness of soul. I know for sure that I have shed enough tears on the issue of singlehood to fill a manmade pool. Even though I am not able to say so far that the end result has been finding a husband, my prayers have not been in vain; they have resulted in a harvest of righteousness and peace in my life.

I am not some super-spiritual woman. I do not have super powers. I am simply a woman who has chosen to find my strength, my joy and my full life through God. I had to learn to be a prayer warrior and, like Jacob, to be willing to fight it out with God, all night if need be, to remain true to Him.

Celibacy has consistently driven me to my knees like nothing else has. It has taught me the meaning of persevering, persisting, and not quitting. At times the pain that I was enduring with being celibate was so unbearable I would contemplate quitting. But since I knew I did not want to go back to the world, the only escape option was to pray.

One of the darkest times in my walk with God was a period of about three years when I lived in Chattanooga, Tennessee. I remember thinking that God brought me there to die. I call that time of my life the desert years. My heart was rock-hard, and I truly was miserable. During more than a year of that time I was reading my Bible and praying, but getting absolutely nothing from my times with God. The Scriptures did not inspire me or move me. My prayers were little more than rote prayers like the Lord's Prayer. Yet I read and prayed every day because I knew in my heart of hearts that if I stopped I would die. I knew my survival depended on being with God. Prayer sustained me, and I would not be here without it. God eventually came to my rescue and sent me help in the form of Lois Schmidt. She nursed me back to health spiritually and helped me get back on my feet.

The greatest thing I discovered through it all was learning not just to pray but to be intimate with God, in true fellowship with Him. I have learned how to walk with Him in this journey called my life. I have discovered God! He makes me smile. He is the source of my joy and salvation, my rescuer, the one who turns my frown upside down even if my circumstances never change. I can start a prayer in tears and total melancholy, and by the end of the prayer I am singing and rejoicing. I have seen God completely transform my mood and my outlook in a single prayer!

In a world of deadlines, traffic jams, stressful jobs and the busyness of life, it is so easy to feel we really do not have the time to devote to prayer. We want to use the little time we may have to ourselves to unwind, relax, sit in front of the TV and do nothing. Or we may want to use our free time to go out with friends and have fun.

Becoming a prayer warrior and growing in my intimacy with God did not happen overnight. If I wanted to have a great prayer life, I was going to have to be deliberate in making time to spend with God. So I learned intimacy with God by making time to consistently pray through my grief, my heartache, my frustration, my fear, my doubt and my disappointment. Intimacy came from imitating Jesus, who, it says in Hebrews 5:7, "offered up prayers and petitions with fervent cries and tears."

Prayer was not something I did and checked off a list; it was what I did to survive. So when I was too restless to sleep, I got up at 1, 2 or 3 a.m. and prayed. I came home from work and prayed instead of watching TV to unwind. I prayed during the uninterrupted time I had before my roommates came home. When my soul was overwhelmed with sorrow I would go down to the river and spend hours reading, praying and singing. I learned to pray with others over the phone as well as in person. I would end conversations with prayer. This is how I have managed to be celibate and live my life to the full through so many years.

As my intimacy with God grew, my prayers became more powerful and impactful. I learned what it meant to approach the throne of grace with confidence. I made bold requests by praying for the impossible to happen—and saw those prayers answered! When I realized who I was praying to, the Creator of the Universe, I stopped thinking small and asking God for small things. Living a powerful life of impact means approaching God, believing that He can do immeasurably more than all we ask or imagine. I studied out miracles a few years back, and what I came to learn is that in order for a miracle to happen there have to be three things in place:

1. A situation of need
2. A human inability to meet that need
3. A faith that only God can meet the need

Wimpy prayers will not produce miracles! Do not be afraid to ask God for what you really want, no matter how outrageous it may seem. I am amazed when I read in the Bible of Joshua praying for the sun and the moon to stand still so the Israelites could win the battle...and God did it (Joshua 10:12–14). Or Elijah's prayer for three years without rain, and it happened; and then again when he prayed that God would make it rain and *that* happened (James 5:17–18). Those are just a few of the prayers in the Bible that blow my mind. I would not even have asked God for those things because I would not have believed that God would adjust nature just because I asked. But Jesus says, "Ask and it will be given to you" (Matthew 7:7). He did not put any stipulations on that, aside from it being in God's will.

As I started praying for the impossible, I had to resolve to be persistent. I had to take on a fighter's mentality, like Jacob did when he wrestled with God. I had to learn to pray through the discouragement of not seeing certain prayers being answered. A Scripture that has helped me in my resolve to be persistent in the face of discouragement is Luke 4:25--27. Jesus, upon encountering faithlessness from those in His hometown, said:

[...] "I assure you that there were many widows in Israel in Elijah's time, when the sky was shut for three and a half years and there was a severe famine throughout the land. Yet Elijah was not sent to any of them, but to a widow in Zarephath in the region of Sidon. And there were many in Israel with leprosy in the time of Elisha the prophet, yet not one of them was cleansed—only Naaman the Syrian."

What is the point that Jesus is trying to make? That God withheld blessings and healing from His chosen people, Israel, because of their lack of faith. Sometimes it is discouraging when you see the large number of single women who want to be married, beautiful and spiritual women who have been faithful for years. In Elijah and Elisa' time there were many widows and many lepers. What was the difference between the widow of Zarephath and the other widows? What was the difference between Naaman and the other lepers? Their situations changed because of their faith. I do not want to lose out because of my lack of faith. I have kept fighting in prayer because I want my situation to change. I want to be the exception and not the rule. I am confident that I will see my request granted in the land of the living.

Prayer is the key to unlocking life to the full. Allow the trials of your life to help you discover an amazing intimacy with God. Realize that you ultimately determine the impact your life will have by the amount of time you invest in prayer.

Chapter 27: Being in Good Company

Anyone who knows me knows I love the story of Jephthah's daughter in Judges. I shared earlier about her and her amazing commitment to God. One of the things that gave her strength was that she was surrounded by good company, company that supported her and encouraged her to remain true. Let us look again at her story.

> "My father," she replied, "you have given your word to the Lord. Do to me *just* as you promised, now that the Lord has avenged you of your enemies, the Ammonites. But grant me this one request," she said. "Give me two months to roam the hills and weep with my friends, because I will never marry."
>
> "You may go," he said. And he let her go for two months. She and her friends went into the hills and wept because she would never marry. After the two months, she returned to her father, and he did to her as he had vowed. And she was a virgin (Judges 11:36–39).

Jephthah's daughter chose to spend her last days on earth with her girlfriends. They went with her to roam the hills and weep over the fact she would never get married.

In this journey of celibacy, you have got to have friends with whom you can roam the hills and who will weep with you when you are sad about not being married. Most important, you have got to have friends who will support your decision to be righteous and to honor God with your life.

Jephthah's daughter and her friends spent two months together. These women were willing to put their own lives on hold and make time for her. It is interesting to note that the word *friends* was plural and not singular. It was not the daughter and her one girlfriend. Having different types of friendships is healthy and beneficial. It does not say how many of her friends went with her, but I get the sense it was more than two.

In this walk of celibacy, I have been blessed to have a variety of friendships that have supported me throughout my journey. I have lifetime friends whom I know will be a part of my life to the end. Some are scattered in different parts of the country, but despite the distance, we still talk consistently. Others are currently nearby, but whether near or far, we have to make our friendships happen.

I have known some friends for almost fifteen years, while I have met others in the last year or two. Some are married, some have children and some are single. I have older friends like Betty, who is in her seventies. She and I took a trip to Dubai with some others to go visit a friend there. Some of my great friendships are with women who are younger than me. I love these women like my little sisters; we know each other's business and counsel each other. I have had seasonal friendships that were with me and impacted my life at certain critical points. I could not have made it through those times without them. I have different friends for different things; I have friends who are my travel buddies, and others that all we do together is eat and talk. Friendships of every kind are such a blessing.

Everyone needs safe relationships in order to live their lives to the full. My close girlfriends provide my safe relationships. I confide in them my deepest and darkest secrets. They know everything about me. I have let them into my life, and they have let me into theirs. Jephthah's daughter felt comfortable being vulnerable with her friends. She cried with them and they with her. They knew what was going on in her life, and they realized the seriousness of it. That is why they took two months out of their lives to spend with her. She was completely open with them. Jesus told His disciples that He called them friends because they knew His business, and He shared everything He had learned from the Father with them (John 15:15). Friends know each other's business, dreams and goals, and they know the personal things.

In safe relationships you know you will not be chastised or criticized for your decisions. You know you will be listened to and supported. These friends will not sugarcoat the truth but instead will speak the truth to you in love. They will tell you what you need to hear because they want you to succeed in your relationship with God. They will direct you back to God and help you to make your life all about Him. It does not seem as though Jephthah's daughter's friends tried to dissuade her from honoring God or tried to plan an escape route for her to run away from home or from Him. I do not want to be naive and think that the idea of running away did not come up, or that none of her friends tried to talk her into it, but whatever went on in those two months, they were with her to the end. She was committed to her God and they supported her.

I cannot begin to tell you how grateful I am for the multiple friends who have stood side by side with me during the toughest times of my life—friends who it seems never get tired of hearing me repeat constantly the same struggle day after day and year after year. I am eternally grateful for the women who literally just held me when all I could do was cry, for those who prayed and fasted with me and for me when I could not do it for myself. I am grateful for friends who would not let me give up or walk away. These are the types of friends you must have to live the celibate lifestyle successfully, but even more so, to live life to the full.

When Jephthah's daughter and her friends roamed the hills, they undoubtedly made a lot of good memories. They explored and went on an adventure. I envision them probably staying up late talking and then waking back up to talk some more. I can imagine scenes of laughter and fun along with scenes of tears. They probably spent time praying. This time was not necessarily all about Jephthah's daughter, either. Each of the women probably shared about what was going on in her own personal life. They would have counseled and encouraged each other. I know her friends cherished the memory of their last days with their friend for the rest of their lives. I can only imagine what they were like when the time came to return home. I can envision them hugging each other as they walked back into town. And in her final moments as she died, they were there with her to the very end.

This time of being celibate is such an amazing opportunity to make memories with your friends. You can take road trips or travel together, have sleepovers or create your own fun traditions. I cherish memories made with many of my friends during my journey, memories that will last a lifetime and into eternity.

Since "bad company corrupts good character" (1 Corinthians 15:33), that must mean that good company builds up good character. You need godly friends to survive this journey with God. Loners, independent spirits and "I only get along with the opposite sex" types of people may stick around but be miserable to be with, or, worse yet, may not last. If you have issues with any kind of relationships, work hard to resolve them. You need friends to make it to the end. Pray to have friends like Jephthah's daughter had.

Chapter 28: Enjoying Your Life

Life is meant to be enjoyed, and our relationship with God is intended to be enjoyable and not a burden. Celibacy should be a time when you are free from concern, having fun living your life and serving God.

One of the biggest misconceptions about living for God is that it is boring, oppressive and no fun at all. I must admit that for many years as a disciple, this described my life exactly. Through counseling, I discovered that I had to choose whether I was going to live life to the full or complain and be discontent and bitter about where I was. For years I struggled because friends would tell me, "Jacqueline, you just need to be content with the Lord." It would make me so upset because I thought contentment meant giving up my dream.

In reality, I did not know how to be content and yet still have hopes and dreams for my life; I didn't know how to make the most of the life that God had given me. After reading Philippians 4 for years, I finally had an epiphany. I discovered how to find contentment in a practical way, which ultimately helped me enjoy my journey with God as a single woman. Paul says:

> I am not saying this because I am in need, for I have learned to be content whatever the circumstances. I know what it is to be in need, and I know what it is to have plenty. I have *learned* the secret of being content in any and every situation, whether well fed or hungry, whether living in plenty or in want. I can do all this through him who gives me strength (Philippians 4:11–13).

Contentment is not inherited once you become a disciple of Jesus; contentment has to be learned. For years I questioned my love for God and my discipleship because I felt that if I were spiritual and really loved God, I would automatically be content. But even Paul had to *learn* to be content. He was a great man who had a conversation with Jesus, saw amazing things (2 Corinthians 12) and helped countless people in their walk with God, yet he had to learn to be content whatever the circumstances.

This insight into Paul has given me so much peace because it made me realize that contentment is not a feeling but a decision to learn something. There were practical things Paul had to do in order to learn to be content. He outlined them in the previous verses:

Rejoice in the Lord always. I will say it again: Rejoice! Let your gentleness be evident to all. The Lord is near. Do not be anxious about anything, but in every situation, by prayer and petition, with thanksgiving, present your requests to God. And the peace of God, which transcends all understanding, will guard your hearts and your minds in Christ Jesus. Finally, brothers, whatever is true, whatever is noble, whatever is right, whatever is pure, whatever is lovely whatever is admirable-if anything is excellent or praiseworthy—think about such things (Philippians 4:4–8).

The road to contentment begins when we make a decision to rejoice, to be gentle, to be conscious of the presence of God, to not be anxious but instead to pray and petition God with every request, to be thankful and to be deliberate in what we think about. Those are decisions that Paul had to make in every situation, and which led to him learning to be content no matter what. A little later, I will look further into each of these practical decisions.

On my road to contentment, I also had to realize that circumstances need not dictate my enjoyment of life. We so often relate happiness and joy to the situations in which we find ourselves. I am always amazed when I read that Paul learned to be content when he was hungry, when he was in need and in want. We often think that if we were in a "better" situation then we would feel better, look better and be happier. "If I had more money, if I were in a dating relationship or had a spouse, if I had better parents, if I had a better job, if I had a better appearance, if my nose were smaller, if I were in a bigger singles ministry, if there were more potential mates around, if there were more spiritual singles, if I were in a bigger city, if the church leaders did more...then I would be happy, my life would be better, and I would do more."

Ironically, we all know people who have more and yet still are not happy. Look at the lives of most celebrities; they have more money than most of us, but also more problems; they have romantic relationships, but most of their marriages end in divorce; they have more resources but don't do more with them—if anything, they do less. Neither circumstances nor situations determine contentment. Contentment is not a feeling; it is a decision.

The secret of being content lies with God. When it seems impossible to be content due to your situation, you can do everything through God who gives you strength. Ecclesiastes says something very profound:

> Moreover, when God gives someone wealth and possessions, and the ability to enjoy them, to accept their lot and be happy in their toil—this is a gift of God. They seldom reflect on the days of their life, because God keeps them occupied with gladness of heart.
>
> I have seen another evil under the sun, and it weighs heavily on mankind: God gives some people wealth, possessions and honor, so that they lack nothing their hearts desire, but God does not grant them the ability to enjoy them, and strangers enjoy them instead. This is meaningless, a grievous evil (Ecclesiastes 5:19-6:2).

Do you see it? God is the one who enables us to enjoy what we have. True enjoyment is not found outside of God. Paul could be hungry, in want and in need, yet be content because God enabled him to be satisfied. He had God, and God was the source of his happiness. Being content is a state of mind. It is being free from doubt and anxiety. It is knowing that God is the source of strength, joy, comfort and peace, and that He is the one who will provide these things no matter what happens.

Realizing that contentment was learned forced me to take responsibility for my life, my discontentment, my bitterness and my unhappiness. I had to stop playing the victim and blaming God or others for my misery. Once I was able to accept the fact that I was unhappy because of me and that I had no excuse, it empowered me. I had the choice and the ability to enjoy the journey of celibacy and live my life to the full, but I was going to have to change and make some deliberate decisions to be different. Every situation I was in was an opportunity to learn to be free from anxiety and doubt, and to choose contentment.

Paul outlined the practical things that helped him learn contentment. Let us look into each pragmatic step.

1. "Rejoice in the Lord always. I will say it again: Rejoice!"

Learning how to rejoice always, in every circumstance, can only come about deliberately. It is human nature to complain, to be negative and to be dissatisfied. We can become like children when we do not get what we want. We pout, get mad, throw temper tantrums, rebel, become defiant, retreat and become inward focused.

We will never have everything we want, but we have to learn to be satisfied with our situations. Do not let trials disturb your spirit. I had to learn how to sing songs, psalms and hymns to help me rejoice. I had to learn how to focus on the positives rather than the negatives. This does not mean I have to be fake and happy-go-lucky. Instead, it means being honest about what I want and admitting when I am not in need. I know when it is well with my soul. I also had to learn what it really means to praise God. The Psalms are full of examples of how to praise God and rejoice in the Lord.

2. "Let your gentleness be evident to all."

The quality of being gentle has to be learned as well. Jesus said in Matthew 11:29, "Take my yoke upon you and learn from me, for I am gentle and humble in heart, and you will find rest for your souls." Gentleness is synonymous with meekness. A characteristic of meekness is nonresistance. Learning to not fight against God's will leads to rest for your soul. I had to learn to be okay with things not going my way. I had to learn to submit and not always try to fix things or manipulate situations. I had to learn to be still—to wait on God and His timing, His direction, and His way.

3. "The Lord is near."

I have had to train my mind to know that God is always near. This knowledge has helped me be free from anxiety and doubt. Hebrews 13:5 says, "Keep your lives free from the love of money and be content with what you have, because God has said, 'Never will I leave you; never will I forsake you.'"

God is always near. This realization is still a hard one for me. By nature, I am very fearful, and a lot of times I just flat-out forget that God is near. Instead I worry and I start trying to figure out how I am going to make my situation "better." I often have to stop and remember God is near.

4. "Do not be anxious about anything, but in every situation, by prayer and petition, with thanksgiving, present your requests to God."

As was pointed out earlier, prayer is essential. Being able to pray to God about *everything* is absolutely amazing. Pray about the details; pray specifically for solutions; pray about your fears, anxieties, concerns, dreams and desires; pray about your surrender to God and His will. Just pray! The promise God grants us is that His peace, which transcends all understanding, will guard our hearts and minds in Christ Jesus.

I had to learn not only to pray, but to pray with thanksgiving. When I am in my dark moments and really struggling with being single, I have learned to pray prayers of thanksgiving. In these times I do not ask for anything. I just thank God in the midst of the pain. Through these prayers I have discovered joy. Most times, by the end of the prayer I am not crying anymore and I feel super encouraged.

God brings me joy. My thanksgiving prayers do not change my circumstances, but they change my outlook, my disposition and my mood. Deciding to be grateful is important because it helps me become satisfied in my situation.

5. "Whatever is true, noble, right, pure, lovely, admirable excellent or praiseworthy—think about such things."

Paul was very deliberate in what he allowed himself to think about. When we are in situations we hate, it is easy to think negative thoughts. It takes intention to not allow ourselves to think negatively, but instead to think about what is lovely, right and true. If contentment is a state of mind, then controlling what we think about will influence our contentment. I must admit that this is easier said than done. Taking every thought captive and making it obedient to Christ (2 Corinthians 10:5) is a full-time job. How else could Paul be content when he was hungry and in need? He had to think differently to be able to achieve this positive outlook, and so must we.

The key to contentment is knowing I can do everything through Him who gives me strength. I don't need to be in a dating relationship to be happy with my life. I can be content with being single while still having a desire to be married. If you cannot be content in your relationship with the Lord, single or unmarried, you will be unable to be truly content in any relationship. The need that drives us into the arms of some human must be met in the Lord. He is the only one we will ever need for life and godliness. This mindset is so valuable because it helps us not to depend on a person or situation for our happiness. What if that person leaves or cheats on you? What if they die? God must always be the main source of joy in our lives. Then we can enjoy the journey!

VI. Successfully Celibate into Marriage

Chapter 29: God's Design for Marriage

Every Christian who desires marriage needs to know how to be successfully celibate until they get married. To be successfully celibate into marriage means that you make Jesus Lord of every area of your life leading up to marriage. In other words, you make Jesus Lord of your singlehood. You make Jesus Lord of your courting period, when you are romantically interested in someone. You make Jesus Lord of your dating relationship. You make Jesus Lord of your engagement. If you have done all of this, then you will ultimately make Jesus Lord of your marriage. The reality is that not every great disciple will have a great marriage, but a successful marriage starts with each spouse being a great disciple for Christ.

The courting phase sets the tone for the dating relationship, the dating relationship sets the tone for the engagement, and the engagement sets the tone for the marriage. Build each phase wisely upon a solid foundation: Jesus. Before we go into the practical aspects of how this is done, I want to give a very basic outline of God's design of marriage.

Obviously I have never been married, so what I share is based on what I have studied in the Scriptures and discussed with married friends. I am in no way an expert, but I offer this understanding of what the Bible says about marriage in the hope of better equipping you to remain celibate until marriage.

In Genesis it says that God made man and placed him in the Garden with the purpose of working in it and taking care of it (Genesis 2:15). Following that, God said, "It is not good for the man to be alone. I will make a helper suitable for him" (v. 18). So God made woman, His ultimate creation, and the Scriptures go on to say, "That is why a man leaves his father and mother and is united to his wife, and they become one flesh" (v. 24). After making mankind, "God blessed them and said to them, 'Be fruitful and increase in number; fill the earth and subdue it'" (Genesis 1:28).

Based on these Scriptures, we can deduce that God intended marriage for two reasons: companionship and reproduction. The design of marriage in the beginning meant *living with God*, working together as one flesh to care for the land, and multiplying by having children.

Marriage was never intended to exclude God. So simple. Let us look further into each of God's stated purposes for marriage.

1. "Be fruitful and increase in number."

The only way I know of to reproduce and have children is to have sex. God gave humans and animals sexual passions to encourage and promote reproduction. Unlike animals, we have emotions and the ability to experience intimacy. There is a huge difference between sexual passion and true intimacy. Anyone can have sex, but God's way allows humans to experience intimacy. God, having created us with both reason and emotion, designed sex to stay within the confines of marriage. He never intended for us to share our bodies with more than one partner.

I heard something profound in one of the classes at the recent International Singles Conference: Only in God does 1+1=1. Marriage is about two people becoming one. This is a mystery indeed; there are many factors that play a role in this "becoming one" business, and sex is a part of that. God's idea of sex is for it to be the physical expression of two committed people becoming one. Children are the fruit of this union. That is so amazing to me. The problem that came and destroyed God's plan for marriage in the Garden was sin.

In 1 Corinthians 7:2, Paul states, "But since sexual immorality is occurring, each man should have sexual relations with his own wife, and each woman with her own husband." Marriage was not originally intended to be a safeguard from sin, but because of sin and human nature, that is what it has become: a safeguard to enable us to serve God and deal with sexual passions. When we take God out of the picture, what ensues is much immorality. Marriage gives us the ability to satisfy our sexual passions and to experience intimacy in giving ourselves completely to one special person.

The body is not meant for sexual immorality (1 Corinthians 6:13). Our society today puts such a huge emphasis on sex, as if we were made only for that. The world makes it seem as if you cannot live productively without it. It is everywhere; sex sells. You might think you are missing out if you are not engaging in sex. The world greatly cheapens the value of sexual relations and marriage.

In Song of Songs, Solomon describes an intimacy and friendship in marriage that goes beyond the physical aspect of sex. It is wise to wait for a committed marital relationship in which to have intimate relations because it affords you the time to get to know yourself and the person you are emotionally and physically connecting with.

Sex is a key aspect in marriage, but it is not the only ingredient for a successful relationship. God, communication, finances, family, and the many needs each partner has beyond sex are vital elements also. Building a relationship is like building a house. The foundation needs to be laid down first, which is a friendship that revolves around God. Sex is like the furniture in the house, enhancing its beauty. Who buys furniture without first having a foundation to place in on?

God did not make man for sex, but made sex for man. It is beautiful in the right context, but in the wrong context it can be devastating. Remember Amnon, who thought he was in love but really was in lust. Lust and sex can complicate things and cloud our judgment. Remember that God made us to serve Him; even sex should always be about God and the way He intended it to be.

2. "It is not good for the man to be alone. I will make a helper suitable for him."

In the Garden, when God created Adam, He gave him the charge to work the land and care for it. God, seeing that it was not good for man to be alone, made Eve to help him. What was Eve to help Adam with? The Scriptures do not say specifically what she was to help Adam with, but possibly she was to help him with the task that God had assigned to him: working and caring for the land. Maybe her role was to help Adam emotionally, mentally, spiritually or even physically so that Adam could fulfill what God wanted him to do. Their marriage was centered on doing the task that God had assigned. Ecclesiastes 4:9–12 says:

Two are better than one,

because they have a good return for their labor:

If either of them falls down,

one can help the other up.

But pity anyone who falls

and has no one to help them up.

Also, if two lie down together, they will keep warm.

But how can one keep warm alone?

Though one may be overpowered,

two can defend themselves.

A cord of three strands is not quickly broken.

God gave Eve strengths and gifts that would help Adam greatly in bringing a good return for their work. They needed each other to fully take care of what God had given them. Companionship and friendship are at the core of marriage, and are among the vital reasons that God made marriage.

Marriage is a partnership. In the Garden, marriage was not just about Adam and Eve but also about the job they had to do. God's intent never was for the focus to be solely on their relationship. Problems will always arise when the heart in a relationship is not centered on God and completing the tasks He assigns to us. Many relationships go wrong when individuals focus solely on each other rather than working together to be devoted to God. That is what is spoken of in 1 Corinthians 7:

> I would like you to be free from concern. An unmarried man is concerned about the Lord's affairs—how he can please the Lord. But a married man is concerned about the affairs of this world—how he can please his wife—and his interests are divided. An unmarried woman or virgin is concerned about the Lord's affairs: Her aim is to be devoted to the Lord in both body and spirit. But a married woman is concerned about the affairs of this world—how she can please her husband. I am saying this for your own good, not to restrict you, but that you may live in a right way in undivided devotion to the Lord (1 Corinthians 7:32–35).

Married men and women are concerned about the affairs of this world—how they can please their spouses—and their interests are divided. An unmarried man or woman is only concerned about the Lord's affairs. Now in this context, marriage may seem to be a bad thing. If this were the case, though, Christians could never have children because they would not be married. The point is that the temptation in a marriage is to focus on one another, which can lead to forgetting about living in undivided devotion to God and doing the work He calls us to do. Whether single or married, our focus has to be on the affairs of the Lord.

Understanding God's design for marriage is vital for singles. If marriage is in His plan for you, this knowledge will help you build a relationship on a solid foundation long before you say your vows.

Chapter 30: Defining Dating

It is clear that God wants us to be involved in sexual relations only after we are married. However, we still have to date before we get married. There is no end of books, blogs, devotionals and the like on the subject of dating. Everyone seems to have an opinion, and for single people, Christian and non-Christian alike, it is a topic that never gets old. Devotionals about dating are always electric and exciting and the atmosphere is always a buzz. Although this is not a book about how to date, I feel it's important to address this topic because God does have expectations about it.

The Bible does not talk about dating. You will not find any Scripture that specifically deals with the subject. We do, however, have some ideas about godly dating based on different Scriptures that talk about one-another relationships with the opposite sex. How Christians date must be different from how the world dates. We know that God's expectation is for us to be pure and holy throughout the dating relationship all the way into marriage.

All couples are different, and their stories about falling in love are different. I love listening to my married friends' stories of how they met their spouse. It never ceases to amaze me all the different ways people find each other. The moment romance comes into the air in someone's life, it can be a crazy time full of emotions and uncertainty.

Remember that courtship sets the tone for the dating relationship, the dating relationship sets the tone for the engagement, and the engagement sets the tone for the marriage. Even though I have never yet been in a dating relationship, I have learned a lot of lessons about what to do and what not to do through my experience of liking different brothers and watching friends navigate various stages of a relationship. Before we go into some basic principles of dating, we first have to clearly define the different stages that occur, from being single to being in a dating relationship to being married.

When I became a disciple of Jesus, I had to learn to look at things in a new way. Coming from the world, I saw that many things in the church that were very different from what I had always seen with my friends and on TV. When I was a young Christian, the dating culture of my church had a lot of rigid dating rules and practices. Since there were no clearly defined expectations laid out in the Scriptures, I, as a teen, assimilated and conformed to the church's dating culture and traditions without question. That culture became my definition of what "spiritual Christian dating" was.

Several years later when my church went through a major reform, so did the dating culture. Now the pendulum had swung to the other end of the spectrum. Gone were the rigid dating rules; during that period there was an almost free, bohemian style of dating. Everyone did as they saw fit. Now what was I to believe? Was this new style of dating to be considered "spiritual"?

I realized at that point that I was going to have to build my own convictions using the Scriptures, counsel and prayer to guide me into what was best. In considering the right and wrong of dating, I had to learn the difference between what was opinion and what the Bible says. I had to clearly understand the distinctions between friendship, dating and marriage. In the world, the boundaries between these three stages of a relationship can be very vague and undefined. For instance, people can live together without being married. Or they are not "officially" in a relationship; they are "friends with benefits." Huh? What is that? How do you know what to expect when there is no clearly defined outline of the relationship?

This vagueness can also be seen in the church; it just looks a little different. We go out together every week and spend a lot of time together, but we are not dating; we are just friends. We are not on a date; it is a "hangout." I have discovered that knowing the difference between the three stages of a relationship has allowed me to be clear on what I should expect and what the appropriate role is in each stage.

Friendship means two people are friends and there is general brotherly love for one another as Jesus commands. Friendship has no agreement to be exclusive. I can have as many friends as I want; the same goes for the other person. There is generally a mutual understanding and expectation that there is no romantic agenda involved.

Dating relationship means two people have *made an agreement* to be exclusive and to invest in a romantic relationship. The investment includes their time, their hearts, their emotions and their affections.

Marriage differs from dating in that two people have *made an agreement and vow* before God and others to love and be devoted exclusively in heart, body and soul to one another until death, to become one and to grow together as one.

How much time, how much emotion, and how much of my affection I invest in each of these stages will look different based on *the nature of the relationship*. As we proceed I will refer back to these definitions to help us understand the right mindset to have in being successfully celibate through dating and into marriage.

Chapter 31: Basic Dating Principles

To build my convictions on the issue of dating, I searched the Scriptures to find what God's expectations were in regard to romantic relationships, marriages and male-female relationships in general. I studied different couples in the Bible and looked at Old and New Testament examples, such as Jesus' and Paul's interactions with women. In addition to the Scriptures, I sought the counsel of spiritual advisors. I also learned some things through trial and error.

The following principles are what I have discovered through my research and experiences. They are guidelines for any single to successfully be celibate into dating and marriage. What I offer is not an exhaustive list, but some basic principles upon which to build your own convictions.

1. Choose a Christian.

"A woman is bound to her husband as long as he lives. But if her husband dies, she is free to marry anyone she wishes, but he must belong to the Lord" (1 Corinthians 7:39). The Bible is clear: we as singles' have freedom to marry anyone we wish. He can be tall; he can be short. He can be from the same race as we are, or a different race. He can be rich or he can be poor. He can be big or small. Whatever we desire, he can be. What freedom! There is only one stipulation: *he must belong to the Lord.* This is not an opinion or a suggestion, but a clear command from God.

This command brings up the question, "How do you know if the person you are interested in belongs to the Lord?" I have seen many Christians all of a sudden become very confused when confronting this issue. Without going into a dissertation on sound doctrine, everything boils down to what the Bible teaches about salvation. How does someone come to belong to the Lord? Acts 2:38 says, "Repent and be baptized, every one of you, in the name of Jesus Christ for the forgiveness of your sins." Has this person repented and made Jesus Lord of their life and been baptized for the forgiveness of their sins? Do they believe this is necessary for salvation? Are they living the lifestyle of a disciple of Jesus? On these issues there can be no compromise.

2. Have a spiritual Naomi.

The love story of Boaz and Ruth would not have been complete without Ruth's mentor, Naomi. I have learned that I need to have an older woman in my life guiding and directing me, to help me know what to do and what not to do with my interest in a man. I find it interesting that once Boaz knew that Ruth was interested, that brother made sure that the matter got settled quickly. From his response (Ruth 3:10), you can tell that he did not think she would be interested in him because of his age. Naomi made sure that Ruth made her intentions clear to Boaz.

Ruth did everything Naomi told her to do, even if it did not make sense or was frightening to her. God blessed her obedience. When it comes to matters of the heart, people can be very defensive and really not be open to seeking or taking advice. Proverbs 12:14 says, "There is a way that appears to be right, but in the end it leads to death." When emotions come into the picture, they can cloud our judgment so that we lose objectivity about a situation. Love is blind, and many times we can be blind to things that are obvious red flags to others.

The heart behind seeking advice should be finding out what the Lord wants. Getting advice is not about getting permission. Our hearts need to ask, "God what do *you* want me to do?" Once you get advice, go back and pray about that advice: "God, is this what you want me to do?" I truly believe that Ruth and Boaz's love story would have never happened if Ruth had not had Naomi in her life. Seek counsel and pray a lot when discovering whom God has in store for you.

3. Build healthy friendships with the opposite sex.

Just as a body, though one, has many parts, but all its many parts form one body [...] Even so the body is not made up of one part but of many [...]

The eye cannot say to the hand, "I don't need you!" And the head cannot say to the feet, "I don't need you!" On the contrary, those parts of the body that seem to be weaker are indispensable, and the parts that we think are less honorable we treat with special honor. And the parts that are unpresentable are treated with special modesty, while our presentable parts need no special treatment. But God has put the body together, giving greater honor to the parts that lacked it, so that there should be no division in the body, but that its parts should have equal concern for each other (1 Corinthians 12:12-25).

We need the brothers, and they need us! The Bible says that no part can say it does not need any other. It even says, "The head cannot say to the feet..." Now, who is the head? Jesus. The feet could be looked at

102

as the least important part of the body. Even Jesus would never say to the least of us, "I do not need you!" How amazing!

Having healthy relationships with the opposite sex is necessary, as the Scripture above testifies. Developing spiritual, platonic relationships does not always come naturally and can be hindered by many things, like our own insecurities, issues with the opposite sex, inexperience and worldliness. For many years in my discipleship, I saw the brothers as dating objects. I would only genuinely be interested in spending fellowship time with brothers who appealed to me and whom I could potentially see myself dating. In addition to a warped view of the men, I also had my own insecurities and inexperience which contributed to me being awkward or weird around them.

A few years ago I realized that if I wanted to enjoy celibacy and have life to the full, I needed to have great friendships with brothers. Without the influence of godly, spiritual men in my life, men in the world started looking a lot more appealing to me, and I was tempted to compromise. I needed my girlfriends, but I also needed healthy male friendships with godly men to support me and keep me focused.

In my search for renewal of mind regarding the brothers, I came across two Scriptures that inspired me and gave me guidelines for what healthy friendship with the opposite sex looks like:

Love must be sincere (Romans 12:9).

[Paul to Timothy]: Treat [...] younger women as sisters, with absolute purity (1 Timothy 5:1–2).

After reading these two Scriptures, my prayer became, "God, help me to love the brothers with a sincere heart and with absolute purity." God started helping me to grow in just loving the brothers and encouraging them without any expectations. From the friendships I built, I learned how to be myself and be comfortable around guys. I learned about men and how they think. They became sounding boards on many different subjects. They encouraged me and gave me words of affirmation when I needed it.

Now, this did not all magically happen. I had to be purposeful and put thought and effort into it. I started with the prayer I mentioned above. I also asked God to build my male friendships. At every meeting of the body, I made it a point to have a great conversation with at least one

103

brother. I would pray for the brothers and the things that were going on in their lives, and when I got an opportunity I would follow up with them. I verbalized to them that I was working on and praying about having great friendships, so they knew I was interested in getting to know them. I made it a point to be at fun activities like birthday dinners and parties, game nights and church sports activities, regardless of whether I felt interested or not. I opened up my home to host events as opportunities to develop friendships. I was flexible with my schedule to make time for dates, and tried really hard not to turn them down unless I absolutely had to.

God has answered my prayers, and I truly have some amazing, healthy platonic friendships with brothers. It is such a privilege and a tremendous blessing to have godly men in my life. I have come to learn that the scripture about the parts of the body in 1 Corinthians 12 is so true: we need the brothers and they need us!

This principle is also important in building a great foundation for a dating relationship. A close friend of mine recently shared with me that if I ever hoped to be married, how could I build a romantic relationship without a foundation of friendship first? Perhaps my future husband would come from my pool of friendships.

4. Guard your heart.

Once I was speaking to a friend and confiding in her that I had an interest in a brother. Her response to me was, "You really need to guard your heart." I left that conversation feeling a little discouraged, apprehensive and cautious. But later I started asking myself what that meant. In the past, when I would hear that phrase, "Guard your heart," I interpreted it to mean be very careful, be cautious, be guarded and withhold your heart.

The Bible does say in Proverbs 4:23, "Above all else, guard your heart, for everything you do flows from it." As I started to ponder this, I could not get my heart to accept that the Bible was advocating that I withhold my heart. Jesus' relationship with Judas contradicted that. If anyone had a reason to guard his heart, it was Jesus. He knew from the beginning that Judas was going to betray Him and ultimately would lead Him to His earthly demise. Yet He gave His heart to Judas freely. He washed his feet, and when Judas came to betray Him, He still called him friend. Jesus treated him as such and loved him as much.

So what does the Bible mean when it says to "guard your heart"? I found my answer in Philippians 4:

Rejoice in the Lord always. I will say it again: Rejoice! Let your gentleness be evident to all. The Lord is near. Do not be anxious about anything, but in every situation, by prayer and petition, with thanksgiving, present your requests to God. *And the peace of God, which transcends all understanding, will guard your hearts and your minds in Christ Jesus* (Philippians 4:4–8, emphasis added).

God's peace guards our hearts and our minds. We get that peace and protection through prayer and petition, with thanksgiving. When we guard our hearts the way the Bible teaches, through prayer and petition, we are able to give our hearts freely to others and live life to the full as God intended.

When God's peace is guarding our hearts, we are able to rejoice, to be gentle, to serve God with gratitude and not be anxious. It removes insecurity and allow us to be free to be our true selves without fear of rejection. It takes away the awkwardness and weirdness that can sometimes occur in the difficult early stages of romantic interest. Staying in a place of uncertainty out of fear of rejection does not guard our hearts, but if we do what Philippians 4 tells us, God's peace will guide us and guard our hearts and our minds.

5. Find security in God (do not compare yourself with others).

I have learned that, realistically, there is always a possibility that other sisters, including friends, will be attracted to the same person I like. The types of men I tend to be attracted to are also attractive to other women: strong, funny, sharp men with confident personalities. We sisters can breed a lot of insecurities and worldliness among ourselves if we are not careful.

In my singles ministry, without exaggeration, the women are spiritual, beautiful inside and out, and have great things going on in their lives. This has caused my insecurities to rise like nothing else has done. At one point, a friend and I liked a brother at the same time. I was so insecure and did so much self-righteous comparing that I felt that he could not possibly pick her over me. It caused a rift between us. Since I had liked him first, I felt she had betrayed my confidence by liking him also, and it damaged my trust in her. Instead of handling it maturely, I avoided conflict. I did not talk about it, but allowed the issue to slowly pull us apart.

In the end he chose neither of us. Sadly, she took it really hard. She eventually left the church and dated and married someone who was not a Christian. I wonder how different things would have been had I been honest with her and had a spiritual perspective about the matter.

With another brother, there was a lot of uncertainty regarding his relationship with his ex-girlfriend, who was part of the same singles ministry. I did not know exactly what the nature of their relationship was; this made me feel weird and uncomfortable around the sister, and I had to fight to just trust God. Eventually, through prayer and casual conversation with him, I sought to learn the nature of that relationship so I could get clarity. The truth then set me free.

The bottom line is that I have had to simply accept the fact that what is for me is for me. No one sister deserves a relationship more than any other. God has a plan, and I have to be still and patient, trusting that He determines my portion, my cup and my boundary lines, which He promises have fallen for me in pleasant places (Psalm 16:5–6).

6. Let the man lead.

In today's culture, some women have become very bold, brazen and aggressive in their pursuit of men. If a woman wants a man, she might walk straight up to him, ask for his number and even offer to sleep with him. I see this straightforwardness in Proverbs when it describes the "adulterous woman":

Then out came a woman to meet him,

dressed like a prostitute and with crafty intent.

(She is unruly and defiant,

her feet never stay at home;

now in the street, now in the squares,

at every corner she lurks.)

She took hold of him and kissed him

and with a brazen face she said:

"Today I fulfilled my vows,

and I have food from my fellowship offering at home.

So I came out to meet you;

This describes many of us before we became Christians. We were pretty straightforward and would go out looking for the guys. Now as disciples, many of us may still have this type of attitude. We may not be as brazen as the woman in this Scripture, but we can become very manipulative and controlling. It is not the brothers pursuing us, but us pursuing them.

You can be doing way too much in pursuit of a relationship, even if you are not being overtly seductive: You set up all the dates and hangout times. You are the one trying to make things happen. You bend over backwards to try to make someone like you more. My sinful tendency is to be this type of woman. I did not even realize that I was doing it. I had no real concept or understanding of courtship and letting a man pursue me. I would go out of my way to be accessible, rather than let the brother woo me.

I have come to realize that the courtship phase is oh so important. It truly sets the tone for the relationship. I was so afraid of being single that I would manipulate situations rather than be still and let God work things out. I did not understand my value—that I was worth being pursued. The Bible says, "He who finds a wife finds what is good and receives favor from the Lord" (Proverbs 18:22). It does not say, "She who finds a husband," or even, "Whoever finds a spouse." The man should be the one doing the searching and pursuing.

I once did a study of all the different marriage relationships in the Bible: Abraham and Sarah, Isaac and Rebekah, Jacob and Rachel, Moses and Zipporah, and Joseph and Mary, to name a few. One of the consistent themes I noticed is that when the men looked for their wives, they found them working and doing what they were supposed to be doing. None of these women were on the hunt to find a man. Letting the men lead means trusting God with the details and being patient—even Ruth was doing this.

7. Trust God with the details.

One of the stories in the Bible that I love and that amazes me is the relationship of Isaac and Rebekah. Abraham was growing old and he did not want Isaac to marry one of the local Canaanite women, out of obedience to God. So he had his servant promise to find a wife for his son from among Abraham's relatives. Abraham told the servant that God would take care of the details: "[…] he will send his angel before you so that you can get a wife for my son from there" (Genesis 24:7). Abraham believed that God was in the matchmaking business.

When the servant got into town, he prayed, and before he even finished, the first woman who approached him was Rebekah. It turned out that Rebekah was from the same family as Abraham. Through answering his prayer, God made it clear to the servant that she was the one. He was elated and showered her with gifts. He met her family and told them how God had brought everything together. After hearing the story, Rebekah's father and brother exclaimed, "This is from the Lord; we can say nothing to you one way or the other. Here is Rebekah; take her and go, and let her become the wife of your master's son, as the Lord has directed" (Genesis 24:50-51). It was clear to all that this was from God.

The next day the servant stated that he wanted to get back on his way and return, but Rebekah's family wanted her to stay a little longer. They gave her the choice, and she decided to go. What trust in God she displayed! She had never laid eyes on Isaac. She did not know his personality or his character, whether he was mean or nice. She did not know his sinful nature, or his strengths and weaknesses. She did not know if she would be physically attracted to him, or he to her. She did not know if their personalities would complement each other, or how well they would get along. All this woman knew was that God was working. A man's prayer and a series of events orchestrated by God revealed that this man Isaac, whom she did not know, was the one chosen for her.

It all ended as a beautiful love story: "Isaac brought her into the tent of his mother Sarah, and he married Rebekah. So she became his wife, and he loved her; and Isaac was comforted after his mother's death" (Genesis 24:67). Did you catch that? He loved her. Rebekah had no pertinent details about Isaac other than that God had made it clear that this stranger was to be her husband. Yet in the end he loved her.

When it comes to romantic relationships we, like Rebekah, have to make a decision to trust God with the details. We have to believe that God is our matchmaker and that He will send His angel to lead that brother to us. There was a lot of praying going on during this time. Abraham was praying. The servant was praying. For all we know, Isaac was probably praying too, since he was in the field meditating when Rebekah arrived. We also need to do a whole lot of praying for God to reveal whom He has set aside for us.

Sometimes we women can be very rigid and just not open to what God may be trying to do. We think that we or the brothers need to have all the ducks in a row, or that we need to know every detail of everything before we can make the decision to give our hearts. Pray and trust God that He, not you, will bring everything together. Just be open and give your heart, and you might well be amazed at what God will do.

8. Be patient.

During the courtship and dating phase, being patient is key. In 1 Corinthians 13:4, the first descriptor of love is "patient." This makes me think of Rachel and Jacob in Genesis 29. Jacob, not Rachel, set the terms of how long their relationship would go on before they got married, which was seven years. What did that mean for Rachel? She had to wait seven years for the next phase of their relationship. That is a really, really long time to like someone.

What in the world did Rachel do during those seven years? She lived her life and continued doing what she was doing: tending sheep. Then after the seven years finally ended, her sister, and not she, got married to Jacob and got to sleep with him first. I can only imagine what was going through Rachel's heart and mind during this time. I would have been beside myself. In the end, she had to trust God to work it out.

Sometimes a brother can take a really long time to ask a sister to be his girlfriend or wife. Or maybe the Christian man of our dreams enters into a dating relationship with another sister, and we feel like it is the end of the world. This scenario can create a lot of anxiety, fretting, worry and uncertainty. However, we have to trust God with the details, and wait patiently. Rebekah's story happened very fast—literally overnight. Rachel's story happened very slowly. It is not up to us to decide which way our stories will unfold.

Amnon was not interested in waiting, and wanted things to happen sooner rather than later. He raped Tamar, and we know that he really felt lust, not love, for her. When you are caught up in the throes of romance you can think you really love someone, when in actuality it is nothing more than lust. Being willing to wait is such a strong display of love; it actually makes the relationship more secure. Being hasty and rash has led to many disastrous relationships and failed marriages. Be patient. Wait on God. Do not take matters into your own hands. Be a daughter of Sarah and "do what is right and do not give way to fear" (1 Peter 3: 6). Let God bring everything together.

I shared at the beginning of this chapter that this is by no means an exhaustive list of dating principles. There are probably more principles that may apply. The point is, each of us has to turn to the Scriptures to build our own convictions regarding dating. If you really want to know God's will for you and how you should date, look to His Word for guidance and pray for His answers. Jesus promises that those who hunger and thirst for righteousness will be filled (Matthew 5:6). May you be filled!

Chapter 32: Cultivating Self-Control

Treat younger men as brothers, older women as mothers, and younger women as sisters, with absolute purity (1 Timothy 5:1–2).

The instruction that was given to Timothy in dealing with younger women was to treat them like sisters with absolute purity. "Absolute" is such a strong word; it conveys a "must," a necessity—no room for excuses or other options.

This should describe our relationships with the opposite sex: brother-sister relationships that are absolutely pure. This command is not difficult when you are not attracted to someone. It is easy to look at a man as a brother if you do not find him physically appealing. It is another thing entirely when you are attracted. God expects absolute purity, without even a hint of sexual immorality or impurity (Ephesians 5:3). It *is* possible to be absolutely pure when you are romantically attracted to someone, but it will require a lot of self-control. Cultivating self-control is essential to the celibate lifestyle for friendship, courtship and dating, and it sets up a strong foundation for great marriages.

Joseph, in Genesis 39, was in a situation where his master's wife was constantly putting sexual pressure on him. At one point she grabbed him and begged him to sleep with her. He could not avoid being around her, since in essence she was in authority over him and she was not going to go away. But Joseph feared God and had deep convictions about doing what was right. He carefully avoided being around her and was even willing to run away from her for righteousness' sake. While he was falsely accused, his self-control helped him stand right before God, which is all that mattered in the end. In other words, he set boundaries for himself so he would not sin. Like him, we have to know ourselves and realize what temptations we can and cannot handle. There are times when we need to establish boundaries to enable us to be right before God.

Self-control is necessary in every stage of a romantic relationship. We need it to help us to be righteous physically with our sexual passions, and to help us be righteous in our thinking. We need self-control emotionally when our feelings are all over the place. Self-control makes it possible for us to say no to our desires in order to live the righteous life that God wants for us.

Even though I am talking about self-control in the context of romantic relationships, it is just as necessary for the Christian walk overall. Self-control is one of the fruits of the Spirit (Galatians 5), and in 2 Peter we are commanded to add self-control to our faith. So whether you are interested in marriage or not, cultivating self-control is a necessity in living for God.

As I grow in my self-control, I am learning that I cannot have everything I want whenever I want it. Part of self-control is being able to delay gratification. Sexual desires are real; they are from God, and we will have them when we are romantically and physically attracted to someone. Too often we think we have to go to the extreme of shutting that part of our lives down completely. But God says "avoid sexual immorality," not "avoid attraction to the opposite sex." Mature self-control means recognizing your desires and putting them in their proper place, not ignoring them. Remember from Chapter 9 that our bodies naturally burn with passion. That is why it is so necessary to learn and practice self-control.

There are several ways in which I am learning how to increase my self-control. The first is praying to be filled with God's Spirit. Since self-control is a fruit of the Spirit, I need the Spirit's help in order to be self-controlled. Second, I am learning the need for self-awareness. Self-awareness and self-control go hand in hand. In 1 Peter 4:7 it states, "Be clear-minded and self-controlled," and in 5:8 it says, "Be self-controlled and alert." Self-awareness is about being clear and alert. Am I clear about what I need and what I want? Do I know what is going on with me? I have to ask myself, "Where am I today and how am I feeling? How am I doing right now? How am I really feeling about being single? What are my emotional and spiritual needs? What do I need physically right now?" Often I am not aware of where I really am emotionally and physically. I can ignore feelings of fear, inadequacy and insecurity, and just keep going as if nothing is wrong—until I crash with an emotional breakdown, have an emotional outburst, or act out by sinning.

A large part of winning the battle for self-control is just acknowledging and being open about what we are feeling and thinking. Many times we do need moments of reflection to truly discover where we stand, but once we identify a problem, bringing it into the open and talking about it makes a huge difference. We need to acknowledge, "I am feeling frustrated and impatient right now with being single"; "I am feeling lonely and really craving intimacy and being held by someone"; "I want what I see everyone else has: holding hands with someone, kissing someone"; "I just feel like having sex right now"; "It was a hard day at work and I just want to escape and feel good and not have to deny myself"; "I do not feel pretty today and I want attention"; "I want to feel good about myself." I cannot control what I am not aware of. Knowing myself and my triggers is vital for cultivating self-control. Being self-aware and honest about your sexual temptations, frustrations, insecurities, fears, desires and wants will help guide you in being self-controlled with your romantic interest.

Once we are more self-aware, the next step is to make plans to address our needs. Make provisions in advance that will help you resist when that desire arises. For example, be aware of the times and places in which you tend to struggle more with your sexual desires. Have a plan for how you will keep yourself active and busy during those times. Be disciplined in going to bed on time and waking up on time, and do not linger in bed unnecessarily.

Here is an example about how being self-aware and having a good plan can help you battle your sexual temptations: "I am feeling really lonely today. Okay, that is identified. Now what am I going to do about that? Let me pray. Let me meet up with or talk to one of my safe relationships and open up about this." Have a plan. Do not ignore what you are feeling. Address it and deal with it. Joining a sexual purity group and having accountability is very helpful in the process of being self-controlled.

Sometimes we can act out our sexual desires by masturbating, watching pornography, or fantasizing in order to deal with our unmet needs. As singles, we can think that if we get married, all of our problems with impurity will end. That is not true. Self-control is a character issue. If you lack self-control as a single, you will lack self-control in your dating relationship and in your marriage. If your needs are not being met in your marriage, you will resort back to the way you used to try to meet your needs when you were single. The Romance Writers of America reports that fifty percent of romance readers are married (and that doesn't account for those living with a partner).[7] The issue is not your situation but your character.

One of the great benefits of being celibate is that it teaches us the valuable lesson of self-control. Lack of self-control is self-destructive and very dangerous in relationships. Whenever we give full reign to our emotions, our feelings, our desires and our wants, we can damage those around us and destroy what is good. When we learn self-control it will reward us in many ways and brings about peace and righteousness.

---

[7] "Reader Statistics," *Romance Writers of America*, accessed January 22, 2015, http://eweb.rwanational.org/eWeb/dynamicpage.aspx?webcode=StatisticsReader.

Learning to control our bodies is not easy, because it requires us to deny ourselves what we want in the moment to gain something better in the end. Many who struggle with celibacy want what they want when they want it, but life does not work that way, whether we are talking about relationships or anything else. For instance, debt enslaves so many people due to their lack of self-control. In whatever way you struggle with self-control, if you lose the battle, you will eventually have to deal with the consequences.

Cultivating self-control is crucial for healthy male-female friendships, courtship, dating and on into marriage. It can be especially important during dating relationships, because your emotions are often all over the place to the point of sensory overload. This is why it is wise to set personal boundaries, which we'll discuss in the next chapter.

Chapter 33: Righteousness in Relationships

The Bible calls us to absolute purity in relationships between men and women, not to make our lives difficult but for righteousness' sake—to not give the devil a foothold. Righteousness is about loving God and wanting to please Him and do what is right in His eyes. We need healthy opposite-sex relationships in our lives, but we also need to be pure. Purity is what helps protect our friendships and other relationships; this does not just refer to sexual purity, but also purity of heart and motive, being sincere in brotherly love. *Love* is the motivation.

For single women, when cultivating self-control there are two areas in which we have to fight daily to be righteous: lust and modesty. Many women assume that lust is just a man's struggle. Lust is a desire to gratify the senses, our bodily appetites. That desire to gratify can motivate us to be impure. For women, lust often takes the form of daydreaming and fantasizing. Jesus addresses the issue of lust:

> "You have heard that it was said, 'You shall not commit adultery.' But I tell you that anyone who looks at a woman lustfully has already committed adultery with her in his heart. If your right eye causes you to stumble, gouge it out and throw it away. It is better for you to lose one part of your body than for your whole body to be thrown into hell" (Matthew 5:28–29).

If looking at someone lustfully means a man has committed the act of adultery in his heart, then for a woman, fantasizing means the same thing. From the heart come evil thoughts (Matthew 15:19). As I shared earlier, I was addicted to daydreaming that led to fantasizing. I used to explain it away by saying I had an imaginative mind. My thoughts were not always filled with sex, but rather storybook fantasies of being pursued and swept off my feet, but they would always eventually lead to impure, sexual thoughts.

To truly pursue righteousness and repent of my lust, I had to dig into my past. I had learned as a child to deal with my pain, insecurity, anger, frustrations, disappointments and fears by daydreaming. At first, I thought it was okay because I would daydream about make-believe characters and celebrities. I realized it was getting worse when I started having impure thoughts about my brothers in the church. I saw that it would only be a matter of time before I was acting out my thoughts on someone real. Adultery and sexual immorality always start off with lustful thoughts. Sin hardens our hearts; righteousness protects our hearts.

Sometimes we can mistake lust for love. Two very different men in the Bible, Amnon and Jacob, thought they were "in love," but only one of them loved in a righteous way:

> In the course of time, Amnon son of David fell in love with Tamar, the beautiful sister of Absalom son of David.
>
> Amnon became so obsessed with his sister Tamar that he made himself ill. She was a virgin, and it seemed impossible for him to do anything to her [...]
>
> But he refused to listen to her, and since he was stronger than she, he raped her (2 Samuel 13:1–14).

> Jacob was in love with Rachel and said, "I'll work for you seven years in return for your younger daughter Rachel" [...]
>
> So Jacob served seven years to get Rachel, but they seemed like only a few days to him because of his love for her (Genesis 29:18–20).

Amnon and Jacob treated the women they loved very differently. Jacob, out of his love for Rachel, was willing to work and wait seven years in order to be with her. The Bible says those years seemed like a few days to him because of his love for her. Amnon, on the other hand, was frustrated and impatient because he was lustful, not actually in love. He gave in to his sexual desires in a violent way. *Being willing to wait and being patient distinguishes between love and lust.*

If lust is the desire to gratify the bodily appetites, then whenever we give in to sexual thinking, masturbation and the like, we are being lustful. If you do not have deep convictions about God's standard of purity now while you are single, you will not have strong convictions when you are in a dating relationship or in your marriage. Just as the true test of love is committing to wait until marriage for sexual relations, the true test of love for God is waiting for Him to fulfill your desires, rather than devising an alternate plan yourself. Perhaps the reason so many marriages end in divorce today is that people are unwilling to wait on God and wait until marriage for sex. Many think they are in love when they are really in lust and, like Amnon, end up hating the other person with intense hatred.

The other area of righteousness that single women must fight for is modesty, which is often overlooked. A few years ago, I heard the most convicting lesson ever about modesty. A sister was teaching the lesson, and in the middle of it she had her boyfriend come in and share from a brother's perspective. His testimony changed my life and deepened my conviction about the need to be modest.

He started by saying that every individual was responsible for their own sin before God. But in the world he had to fight to protect his eyes from the way women presented their bodies. He found it so discouraging to come to church and still need to fight to protect his eyes because of what sisters were wearing. There were even times when he did not want to come to church at all because he did not want to sin against God by struggling with lust due to what he saw. He came to the conclusion that he would not fellowship with sisters who were dressed immodestly because he would not jeopardize his relationship with God for the sake of being nice. He always wanted to be with a woman who was modest, and that was one of the reasons he was initially attracted to the sister who became his girlfriend.

Remember that one of the definitions of purity is "freedom from guilt or evil; innocence." Modesty is an important aspect of purity and righteousness because we want to be innocent of causing another to sin:

> **It is God's will that you should be sanctified: that you should avoid sexual immorality; that each of you should learn to control your own body in a way that is holy and honorable, not in passionate lust like the pagans, who do not know God; and that in this matter no one should wrong or take advantage of a brother or sister. The Lord will punish all those who commit such sins, as we told you and warned you before. For God did not call us to be impure, but to live a holy life (1 Thessalonians 4:3–7)**

God says on the issue of purity that we must not wrong a brother or take advantage of him, and one of the ways we do that is through being immodest. I was cut to the heart after hearing the brother's testimony because I never knew that my brothers, God's sons, would struggle with coming to church as a result of what I chose to wear. God calls us to be modest not for His sake but for the sake of the men. Men are visual creatures, and we can easily lead them to sin because of how we dress. We want to be desired and attractive, but being immodest is the way that the world goes about fulfilling that desire. A godly woman chooses to make herself attractive by fearing God (1 Peter 3:1–6), and a godly man will be looking for a godly woman.

Modesty is one of those issues that can stir up a lot of controversy among the sisters. What exactly is considered immodest can be very subjective. A Scripture that has helped me is 1 Timothy 2:9–10: "I also want the women to dress modestly, with decency and propriety, adorning themselves, not with elaborate hairstyles or gold or pearls or expensive clothes, but with good deeds, appropriate for women who profess to worship God." What I wear is a part of my worship to God. My clothes are just as important as the singing, praying, communion, contribution and sermon of a regular worship service. It is a part of my spiritual act of worship to God.

Three things should describe our dress: modesty, decency and propriety. A little acronym that I use to help myself and other sisters when questions arise about an outfit is MDP: Is it modest? Is it decent? Is it proper? Modest simply means not revealing or discreet. Decent means fitting, meaning it fits properly; not too tight or too short. Propriety means it is respectable and in good taste. At the time when Paul wrote this letter to Timothy, braided hair, gold, pearls and expensive clothes were reflective of pagan women's dress. When you think of movies that reflect the era of Jesus' time, the attire for both men and women was very covered-up. I never saw braided hair, gold, pearls or expensive-looking clothes. That was not the attire of the Jews. The Gentiles were the ones who wore the braided hair, gold, pearls and expensive clothes. Today these articles are not associated with bad taste. However, when you see movies and videos of today that reflect the world, what do we see? Scantily-clad women, short shorts and see-through outfits, blouses that expose a woman's bust, tight jeans and the like.

Modesty and purity may seem confining, but they actually bring freedom. Choosing to be righteous in our relationships will bring about a great reward and help establish those relationships on a strong foundation. Building any relationship on the rock of Jesus' words does not mean that the relationship will not face troubles, problems or pain, but it does mean that it will weather the storms and still remain standing.

Chapter 34: Knowing the Boundaries

When it comes to the journey from singlehood into a Christian dating relationship and marriage, there can be many different interpretations of what is appropriate and what is not appropriate. Many things can influence someone's views on dating, such as religious background, societal culture, family upbringing and church culture. These views can vary from rigid rules to no boundaries at all. Lack of expectations can create chaos in a relationship. There is wisdom in establishing clearly defined expectations, but setting rules can become legalistic, and can turn out to be unrealistic in practice. Neither extreme is good, and finding the healthy balance is not always easy. So how do we approach the subject of what is appropriate and what is not in dating?

We have to begin by realizing that boundaries and rules are two different things. *Rules* are set, prescribed, habitual practice, usually made by someone in authority. The same rules go for everyone under that authority, no matter the person, situation or circumstance; they usually do not allow for variations or variables. *Boundaries* are borders, limits or barriers. Boundaries will vary from person to person and are not prescribed by someone in authority. Boundaries will also vary within someone's life based on changes of season and circumstances. Unlike rules, they are not rigid or set. We establish boundaries with the end goal of being holy; setting boundaries, rather than making up rules, is better way to approach dating because it allows for specific limits that will best suit each person and situation to help us be holy before God.

God provides some insight into how we should set our personal boundaries:

It is God's will that you should be sanctified: that you should avoid sexual immorality; that each of you should learn to control your own body in a way that is holy and honorable... (1 Thessalonians 4:3–4).

His will is for people to learn to control their own bodies. By knowing your own limits, you can cultivate self-control and establish boundaries in a way that is holy and honorable. Boundaries should be based on each person understanding what they can or cannot handle, so that they do not violate their conscience or God's commands. Know your limits, know your conscience, and know God's commands and expectations for you. God places the responsibility for doing this on each individual.

While we each need to take responsibility, setting healthy boundaries in every area of our lives is a learned skill and most of us will need help. We may not have the sobriety, maturity or wisdom of knowing ourselves, and we may not know how to put proper boundaries in place in different situations. This lack of discernment is why prayer and advice in your life are so important. We need God and others to show us and teach us what boundaries to put in place and how to do that.

When it comes to setting up boundaries in relationships, I have learned the hard way how being unclear about my expectations and limits, as well as the other person's, leads to consequences for everyone involved. First, I had to learn to be clear on the definitions of a friendship, a dating relationship and a marriage and how they differ, as we have already discussed. Second, I had to learn what boundaries to set for *me* to protect myself and the other person in a relationship.

I took to heart the advice my counselor shared about boundaries in romantic relationships: do not play the role without the title. If my title is not "girlfriend," then I should not be acting like a girlfriend. If my title is not "wife," then I should not be acting like a wife. Knowing the nature of the relationship and what my title is within that relationship will ultimately dictate what my role and actions will be and how I behave in regard to 1) my time, 2) my emotions and 3) my affections. These are the things I have learned to set limits on, based on the nature of the relationship, knowing that each will look different in a friendship, in a dating relationship and in a marriage. Let us take a deeper look into these three areas.

1. Time

In *The 5 Love Languages*,[8] author Gary Chapman defines the different expressions of love in a romantic relationship. Quality time is one "language" that expresses love to many people. Time is a valuable resource of mine, and it is an extension of me. In the past, I have unwittingly spent too much time with men under the guise of being "just friends" without the titles of girlfriend and boyfriend; before I realized it I was emotionally connected, taking things personally and feeling disappointed when the brother did not reciprocate.

I have to set boundaries on how much time I spend talking on the phone with a brother, how much alone time I spend with a brother,

---

[8] Gary Chapman, *The Five Love Languages: How to Express Heartfelt Commitment to Your Mate* (Chicago: Northfield Publishers, 1995).

how much time I physically interact with a brother, and how much time I spend doing encouraging things for a brother who is not my boyfriend or husband. If we both have not agreed to be in a committed relationship, then he should not have much access to my time.

In the Scriptures I have noticed that Jesus rarely spent alone time with women. One of the rare accounts is when He was talking to the Samaritan woman in John 4. This passage notes that the disciples were surprised to find Jesus talking with a woman. Why were they surprised? Aside from the fact that she was a Samaritan, Jesus just did not spend alone time with women, which in Jewish culture was not considered appropriate. Most of Jesus' interactions with people, especially with women, tended to be in groups. There is wisdom in that, because I feel that when people start spending too much alone time with the opposite sex, someone usually starts developing romantic feelings. That is how most affairs start—when people just spend too much time being with and talking to someone other than their spouse.

2. Emotions

I also need to set boundaries on my emotions, my feelings, and the personal and intimate details of my heart. When I start spending too much time with someone, we will eventually start discussing intimate details about each other, and that creates emotional connections. This connection can be harmful outside of a defined romantic relationship.

I have learned that I can be honest about my life and myself without having to go into deeply personal details. How much I share and how deep I go depends on the nature of the relationship. If I am in a friendship with a brother and we have not agreed to be in a committed relationship, then he is not allowed access to the intimate details of my life and my heart.

A great example of healthy emotional boundaries is Jesus' relationship with Martha in Luke 10. Martha was upset with her sister and she felt very comfortable talking to Jesus and being honest with Him about how she was feeling and what she wanted Him to do. I do not see the two of them exiting the premises to have a private conversation about it. I do not see them spending hours discussing the deep and personal details of Martha's heart, her past and her relationship with her sister. I see an honest discussion between friends (Jesus was a family friend)—and nothing more.

My emotions, my feelings and the personal and intimate details of my heart are privileged, valuable possessions, and no one can have access to them without making a commitment to invest in a relationship with me.

3. Affections

Lastly, I have had to set boundaries on my affections, which I will choose to define as the other four love languages. They include my words of affirmation, my acts of service, my gift giving and my physical touch. I have been guilty of overstepping my limits and doing far too much for a man who has not made any agreements to commit to me or invest in a relationship with me. I have given way too many gifts, or excessively elaborate gifts, in the name of being "encouraging" to someone I was attracted to. I have had a hard time keeping my hands to myself and have found reasons to just touch a brother in the name of "fun," when it was really nothing more than flirting. I have gone above and beyond to serve and encourage a brother in the name of "friendship" when the reality was that I was serving because I was attracted; I honestly would not have served any other brother in that manner. When Jesus loved the disciples, He showed His love to all in the same manner. He washed *all* the apostles' feet, even Judas's.

Again, how much of my affection I give must depend on the nature of the relationship. If a brother is not my boyfriend, then he is limited to the same affection I would show any other brother or friend. If he is not my husband, then he is limited to an amount of affection that will protect the purity of the dating relationship.

Knowing how to set boundaries will protect your heart and keep a friendship from going in a direction that would not be pleasing to God. Proverbs 22:3 says that a prudent man sees danger and takes refuge, but the simple keep going and suffer for it. These "love languages" are areas of danger that many singles can wander into, leading to a lot of heartache and grief. These boundaries are not absolutes, but please take time to consider each of the areas discussed and pray about how each of them would look in your own life if your absolute priority is pleasing God. Build your own convictions on the subject. As we go into the next section, on a relationship's development from friendship to the altar, look at these things simply as basic guidelines that may provide some help in your fight to date and marry God's way.

Chapter 35: From Friendship to the Altar

Marriage is a beautiful institution that God has designed for two individuals to become one, share life's journey together, and build a family together. Most people—Christians or not—if given a choice, would choose to be involved in a romantic relationship. But many choose not to be married, not because they do not want to be in a romantic relationship but because they just do not see successful marriages that stand the test of time—even among professed Christians. In a day and age when the institution of marriage has been undermined and undervalued, many do not see the value of fighting to do it God's way from friendship to the altar.

Throughout this book, the consistent theme has been about making Jesus Lord of every area of our lives. Whether you choose to remain single all the days of your life or choose to get married, all that really matters is making Jesus Lord of every step of the journey.

Friendship

Establishing boundaries early in a romantic relationship, as soon as there is an identified attraction on either side, is very important. Sisters often like to take the passive route and leave all the responsibility to the brothers to set the right boundaries. However, God's will is that each person should learn to control themselves. You have to set boundaries for yourself, whether the brother sets his own or not. Standing firm in your boundaries will allow the brother to know how he must proceed in treating you.

Women will be tempted to be insecure, to compromise, to manipulate and to lead at every stage of a relationship. Having a spiritual Naomi, along with much prayer, will be very helpful in guiding you, especially when emotions are running high. Seek clarity to determine if you both have the same expectations, so you can understand the other person's true intention and be on the same page. It is easy to mistake acts of kindness for romantic interest. There are times when a brother may be going out of his way to make you feel special for no other reason than to simply encourage you as his sister in Christ. There are times, however, when he is going out of his way because he is attracted to you. It is easy to confuse the two. Then there are times when brothers may intentionally or unintentionally be sending mixed signals, saying one thing but doing another; many sisters end up disappointed because they were thinking something completely different than what the brother was thinking.

I have had one friendship with a brother I was attracted to that has required me to seek clarity several times. When my counselor advised me to talk to him about where we stood, it was scary to me and I felt uncomfortable bringing it up. I felt like I was being forward and putting myself way out there. I could not bring myself to open up to him, but what I did do was pray a lot about it. I understood the necessity of gaining clarity for my peace of mind but I was just scared, so I prayed that God would work it all out, and that is what God did. The brother casually mentioned how grateful he was for his platonic sister relationships, and included my name in that list. Right then I knew where we stood; he saw me as a platonic friend.

Yet as my friendship with this brother continued, I started sensing a shift and at some point it did not feel platonic anymore. Again, my counselor's advice was to gain clarity. I prayed, and this time I brought it up with him. It felt awkward at first, but because we were friends we were able to discuss it and he plainly told me he did not want anything more than just a friendship. That was hard to hear, but now I knew clearly where we stood—but more importantly, where I stood.

Then again, as time went along, I started feeling that he was sending mixed signals. He had clearly stated to me that he did not want anything more than a friendship, but now he was doing and saying things that did not seem platonic and hinted at something more. Again my counselor's advice was to gain clarity and address the issue. Again I prayed and God created an opportunity to bring it up. We were able to discuss it, and even though we had different opinions about what was appropriate in a platonic relationship, I was able to express to him that I could not handle what he was doing. He respected my wishes. We are still great friends and I value his friendship, but we are both clear on boundaries and making sure the friendship looks like a friendship and not a dating relationship.

I do not have a formula for how to have these types of conversations, other than to pray and seek counsel. I was very fortunate to have a professional counselor who is also a disciple guiding me through this process. I would not advise going through this without much prayer and guidance from a spiritual older woman in the Lord. It most likely will feel awkward. You may not hear what you want to hear; you may get your feelings hurt initially, but in the long run it will benefit you, saving you from the pain that comes from feeling misled.

Courtship

Courtship is the time where a brother makes it clear that he is romantically interested in you. From what most men and women have told me, it usually is very obvious when a man is interested because men go after what they want. If a man is attracted to you and wants to be in this kind of relationship with you, he will make it happen. He should be leading the way in making his intentions clear. If the feelings are mutual, then he should be working to win you over.

When setting the boundaries during this stage, you should keep in mind that you are not the girlfriend yet, so you have to conduct yourself patiently, not making yourself too accessible, yet still being a friend. And until you agree to date each other exclusively, your relationship remains only a friendship. Through prayer and your spiritual Naomi's guidance, God will make it all clear when and how the nature of your relationship will change.

Dating and Engagement

Boundaries during the dating relationship and engagement are similar to the previous phases, except that now you have to know your boyfriend's limits and expectations and God's expectation for each of you in the relationship. As I mentioned earlier, each person is different and each couple is different. Therefore, setting healthy boundaries will look different for each couple. For that reason, it is imperative that in a dating relationship there must be much prayer, much counsel and advice, and much communication between the two of you to ensure what will be best for the relationship.

Since boundaries are not set, rigid rules, they may be set differently at different times in the relationship. This flexibility necessitates frequent and open communication. The two of you have to learn to talk to each other about your needs and to make sure those needs are being met in the relationship. If you can successfully establish and maintain healthy boundaries during dating and engagement, you will have a great foundation of healthy communication skills needed for a strong marriage.

The last point I want to make about celibate dating relationships is to remind you to know your role and stay in that role. You are boyfriend and girlfriend, not husband and wife. In the relationship you are not one; you are two separate people with two separate lives. As individuals, you each have your own time, your own emotions and your own affections. As a dating person, you have not made a vow to God to love, serve and give yourself only to the one you are dating. Remember that as an unmarried person, you are to maintain undivided devotion in body and spirit to the Lord. Again, this is where prayer and counsel are key, because as the relationship progresses toward marriage, your connection to one another has to progress as well. How that all happens, when it should happen and in what manner it should happen depends on the couple.

In my twenty years as a disciple, the two things I have consistently noticed that determined success or failure in dating relationships were commitment to prayer and getting advice. Those couples who prayed a lot about the relationship, prayed before making decisions, prayed for God's guidance and generally relied on prayer usually enjoyed their dating relationship and had great victories in their purity. They also were the ones who made it a priority to seek out counseling and advice. Those couples that were not really grounded in prayer and generally did not get advice or put it into practice when given usually were the ones who ended up compromising in their purity, experiencing a lot of "drama," or both.

There is great reward in being celibate God's way until marriage. It is not easy and it is not for the faint of heart, but in the end God is pleased. No one knows the ultimate outcome of the journey of marriage. When you say for "better or worse," you do not know what "worse" will be. Unfortunately, even doing it God's way during each step leading up to marriage does not guarantee that the relationship will never end in divorce or even that it will be a great marriage. The key to a great marriage is for both parties to continually choose to remain faithful and obedient to Jesus as Lord of their life and their marriage. All you can control is yourself and how you will choose to live your life. Trust God and fight to honor Him every day of your life, and in the end you will receive the ultimate reward: eternity with God!

VI. Successfully Celibate until Death

Chapter 36: The Gift

> Jesus replied, "Moses permitted you to divorce your wives because your hearts were hard. But it was not this way from the beginning. I tell you that anyone who divorces his wife, except for sexual immorality, and marries another woman commits adultery."
>
> The disciples said to him, "If this is the situation between a husband and wife, it is better not to marry."
>
> Jesus replied, "Not everyone can accept this word, but only those to whom it has been given" (Matthew 19:8–11).

I used to hear that some will have "the gift" of being single all their lives until they die. Ironically, when most would speak of this "gift" it sounded more like a curse than a gift. In Matthew 19, Jesus does make it clear that not everyone wants or chooses to be married. Some might desire marriage at some point in their lives, but ultimately they are okay just being single; they prefer it that way.

Being celibate is a choice no matter what age you are or where you may be in life. Some may be widowed. Some may have been married and are now divorced. Some, like me, have never been in a dating relationship or married. Some may have left behind the life of homosexuality to follow Christ but genuinely do not have an interest in or attraction to the opposite sex, so they remain single. Some may have been in dating relationships but are now content with singlehood.

Wherever you are, it is okay to be okay with being single. You are not abnormal if you do not desire to be married. Also, you are not abnormal if you do desire to be married no matter what age you are. Committing to being single until death entails embracing the realities of growing older in the Lord as you age physically.

I have at times wondered: If I never get married, what in the world will I do with my life as I get older? Buy a house, maybe, but then what? Care for an aging parent, but when they die, then what? What would my life consist of, really? These are legitimate questions and concerns. What does God expect from the mature older single? Is it possible to truly live life to the full even into your old age? If every part of the body of Christ is needed and important, as it says in 1 Corinthians 12, then there is a great purpose in life that God desires for His older sons and daughters!

The Bible specifically talks about the role of the older women in the church:

> **Likewise, teach the older women to be reverent in the way they live, not to be slanderers or addicted to much wine, but to teach what is good. Then they can urge the younger women to love their husbands and children, to be self-controlled and pure, to be busy at home, to be kind, and to be subject to their husbands, so that no one will malign the word of God (Titus 2:3-5).**

The God-given role of older woman in the church is to live lives worthy of imitation and to train the younger women. The mere fact that you have reached the status of "older woman," whether spiritually or physically, means you have experiences that enable you to teach and train others. There will always be younger women in the church who need your help and would love to have an older spiritual woman in their lives guiding and directing them. Training involves investing in someone. There are many ways to invest in the younger women: you can open your home to spend time with younger sisters; you can write weekly, monthly, or quarterly lessons on different topics like hospitality and the ones mentioned in the Titus scripture, and share them with the younger women; you can converse and pray over the phone. These are a few ideas to get you started. You may not be able to invest in large numbers of women, but even if it's only one younger woman in the ministry, *give*.

Training a younger woman gives you a focus and enhances your relationships and your life. When I think about Ruth and Naomi's relationship, I see Ruth as a blessing to Naomi. Naomi needed Ruth more than she may have initially realized. Naomi, an older widow, was alone. Ruth offered companionship, worked, provided for her and took care of her. Near the end of the book, you see how Ruth grew in her life and brought joy and a sense of family to Naomi as well. Give to the younger women in the church. You never know—these relationships may become the greatest joys and blessings to your life as you get older.

No widow may be put on the list of widows unless she is over sixty, has been faithful to her husband, and is well known for her good deeds, such as bringing up children, showing hospitality, washing the feet of the Lord's people, helping those in trouble and devoting herself to all kinds of good deeds (1 Timothy 5:9–10).

It seems the Bible gives us God's expectations for the older woman: she should be well known for devoting herself to all kinds of good deeds. It seems age is not a factor in being a servant; *all* are expected to serve, including those who are older—this "list of widows" was for single women over sixty. There is no excuse for any disciples not to serve. The call for undivided devotion is the call for all, no matter their age. I appreciate that the Scripture says "all kinds of good deeds." Many things can be classified under that description. Pray and find creative ways to do good deeds within the situation that God has you in. Being celibate until death means anyone can live life to the full and make a great impact well into their old age. Discover God's expectation and see what He has to offer!

Chapter 37: The Reward

I recently went through a really bad spell during which I was tired, weary and fed up with this celibate journey. It had been hard watching close friends date, marry and move on with their lives, buying homes and starting families. I was feeling left behind. I am not always okay with being single, but I am learning to accept God's will and trust that He is my faithful Creator and knows what He is doing with my life. I have my good days and bad my days; recently it has been a season of bad days. On one of these days I just broke down in tears and I prayed, "God, I feel like I made the worst decision in choosing you. I was not expecting for this to be my life. This is harder than I imagined, and I am not sure if I want to do it anymore. Did I make a mistake in choosing you and this life? Show me that I did not make a mistake!" I remember I cried myself to sleep that night with no answer. A few days later, this thought came into my mind, and I meditated on it: "If there is a cost to following Jesus, as He said, then what is the benefit? What is the reward of choosing God and doing things His way?" I decided to start in Romans and go through the New Testament, looking at what is mentioned as the reward. I will share what I found with you. This is not exhaustive, and I only made it to 2 Peter, but when I was finished writing in my journal I had written thirteen pages front and back of Scriptures talking about the reward of having Jesus. Here is a sample of what I wrote down:

Romans 2:7 - Receive eternal life
Romans 5:1-11 - Have peace with God, stand in grace, saved from God's wrath
Romans 6:22-23 - Set free from sin, benefit of holiness, result is eternal life
Romans 8:28-39 - God is for me! God will graciously give me all things. I am justified.
1 Corinthians 2:16 - Have the mindset of Christ
1 Corinthians 6:11 - Get washed, sanctified, justified
1 Corinthians 9:24-27 - Hope of receiving a crown that will last forever!
1 Corinthians 12:27 - Become part of the body of Christ
1 Corinthians 15 - Will be resurrected from the dead and clothed with a spiritual body, immortal, imperishable
2 Corinthians 4 - Have the light of the gospel of the glory of Christ. Have the light of the knowledge of the glory of God in the face of Christ. This is a treasure! To see and know the gospel of Jesus
2 Corinthians 4 - Have all surpassing power within me
2 Corinthians 4 - Inwardly renewed day by day. Eternal glory awaits me! Fix my eyes on what is unseen

2 Corinthians 5:1-10 - Have an eternal house in heaven, built by God. Have the Spirit as a deposit guaranteeing what is to come: to one day be clothed with a heavenly dwelling

2 Corinthians 5 - Become a new creation. My sins not counted against me. In Jesus I've become the righteousness of God

2 Corinthians 6:16 - I am the temple of God, the living God. God lives with me and is my Father

Galatians 3:26 - Become sons of God and have been clothed with Christ through baptism

Galatians 4:7 - I am an heir. God has made me His heir!

Ephesians 1 - Blessed in the heavenly realms with *every spiritual blessing* in Christ. Not the earthly realm but the heavenly realm

Ephesians 1 - Chosen by God

Ephesians 1 - Found to be holy and blameless in God's sight

Ephesians 1 - Adopted as sons through Jesus

Ephesians 1 - Freely given grace

Ephesians 1 - Redemption through Jesus' blood

Ephesians 1 - The forgiveness of sins

Ephesians 1 - Marked in Jesus by the Holy Spirit

Ephesians 1 - Guaranteed an inheritance (not guaranteed a husband or any other earthly blessing but an inheritance)

Ephesians 1 - Become God's possession. Gain redemption

Ephesians 2 - Saved by grace

Ephesians 2 - Raised up with Christ and seated with Him in the heavenly realms!

Ephesians 2 - Become a citizen of God's people

Ephesians 2 - Become a member of God's household

Ephesians 3:12 - Able to approach God with freedom and confidence!

Ephesians 5:8 - I am light in the Lord

Philippians 3 - My citizenship is in heaven. Awaiting a Savior from heaven. Awaiting Jesus to transform my lowly body to be like His glorious body!

Philippians 3:7-11 - Gain Christ! Get to know Christ Jesus, my Lord. Be found in Jesus. Gain righteousness!

Colossians 1:5 - Have a hope that is stored up for me in heaven! Qualified by God to share in the inheritance of the saints in the kingdom of light!

Colossians 1:1-14 - Rescued from the dominion of darkness and brought into the kingdom of Jesus. In Jesus I have redemption and forgiveness of sins

Colossians 1:15-29 - Been reconciled to God. Presented as holy in His sight, without blemish and free from accusation!

Colossians 3 - I can work knowing I will receive an inheritance from the Lord as a reward

1 Thessalonians 1 - I am loved by God! God has chosen me! Jesus rescues me from the coming wrath. Waiting for Jesus from heaven

1 Thessalonians 4 - Dead in Christ and will rise! Will be caught up in the air to meet the Lord! Will be with the Lord forever!

1 Thessalonians 4 - Sons of light and sons of the day

1 Thessalonians 5 - Appointed not to suffer wrath but to receive salvation through our Lord Christ. May live together with Him!

2 Thessalonians 1 - Saved from the punishment for those who do not know God and don't obey the gospel of Jesus. Saved from the punishment of everlasting destruction. Saved from being shut out from the presence of the Lord and shut out from the majesty of His power

2 Timothy - Will receive a crown of righteousness, which Jesus will award, for those who finish the race!

Titus 3 - Justified by grace. Spirit poured out generously on us. Saved. Become heirs having hope of eternal life

Hebrews 10 - Confidence to enter Most Holy Place. Able to draw near to God. Have better, lasting possessions

Hebrews 11 - Heavenly country. God has prepared a city for the saints

Hebrews 12 - Name written in heaven!! Receiving a kingdom that cannot be shaken!

James 1 - Receive the crown of life which God has promised to those who love Him, to those who have stood the test!

1 Peter 1 - Given new birth into a living hope! Given new birth into an inheritance that can never perish, spoil or fade. Kept in heaven for us!

1 Peter 2 - Being built into a spiritual house to be a holy priesthood! Chosen people. Royal priesthood. Holy nation. Belong to God. Receive mercy!

2 Peter 3 - God's promise. Looking forward to a new heaven and a new earth, the home of righteousness

I remember that after writing these Scriptures down in my journal, all I could do was cry, rejoice and praise God! It reminded me of the WHY for doing things God's way: my motivation for submitting to Him, making Jesus Lord, denying myself and taking up my cross daily, waiting on God's timing and accepting His will for my life is so that I can gain Christ and be found in Him. I am striving for my reward and my crown in heaven!

God is faithful, and He does give us the desires of our hearts, but that may not always look like the dream we have envisioned for ourselves. I never in a million years thought that I would still be single after twenty years in the faith. Many times I have come close to losing my inheritance because I was caught up in what I was not getting here on earth, instead of realizing that the true prize is in heaven.

Is celibacy easy? No!! Does it mean that if I choose to do things God's way, I will get a husband? No!! What we are guaranteed is an inheritance in heaven. Fight in such a way and live your life in such a way that you win THAT prize! To God be the glory!